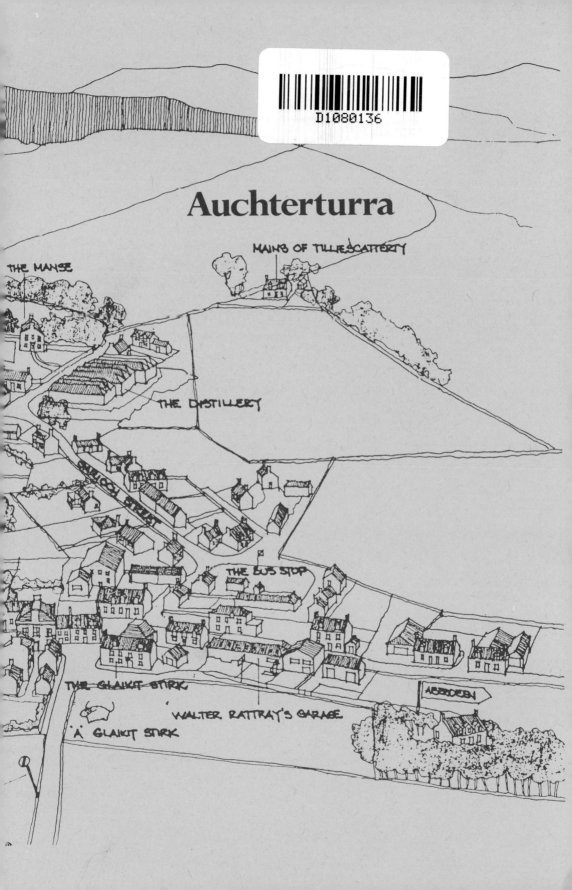

Auchterturra

MAINS OF TILLIESCATTERTY

THE MANSE

THE DISTILLERY

SCHOOL STREET

THE BUS STOP

THE GLAIKIT STIRK

'WALTER RATTRAY'S GARAGE

ABERDEEN

'A' GLAIKIT STIRK

SCOTLAND THE WHAT?

SCOTLAND THE WHAT?

Written by
BUFF HARDIE and STEPHEN ROBERTSON

Lyrics by
BUFF HARDIE

Music by
GEORGE DONALD

Directed for the stage by
JAMES LOGAN

GORDON WRIGHT PUBLISHING
25 MAYFIELD ROAD, EDINBURGH EH9 2NQ
SCOTLAND

British Library Cataloguing in Publication Data

Hardie, Buff
    Scotland the what?
    I. Title II. Robertson, Stephen
    III. Donald, George
    792.9'2   PN6175

    ISBN 0-903065-59-2

PHOTO CREDITS. Page numbers given.
Martin Johnston Ltd: 43, 55, 64, 116, 132, 171, 193, 198, 203, 259.
Gus Christie: 133.
Westland of Inverurie: 79, 85.
Aberdeen Journals: 17, 18, 98.
Glasgow District Council: 16 top.
Grampian Television: 15 top, 49, 154, 239.
Gordon Wright: 14 bot., 16 bot., 30, 32, 77, 87, 111, 112, 123, 125, 142, 145, 151, 164, 176, 179, 189, 205, 207, 208, 215, 218, 225, 228, 233, 241, 244, 251, 254, 257, 266, 269.
Back cover photo: Gordon Wright.
Front cover photo: Photo Express, Edinburgh.
Maps of Auchterturra: Roddy McKenzie.
Music copyist: Isobel Teague.

Typeset by IPEK Origination.
Printed and bound by Billing & Sons Ltd., Worcester.

Contents

Foreword 9

Introduction 11

1973

The Banker.. 19

Father of the Bride... 21

True Love o' Mine 22

Coal.. 24

The Scottish Plumber... 29

The Newspaper... 30

You're the Top 33

Cinemas 34

Bruce and the Spider.. 36

1975

The Will... 39

Our Glens 44

Hospitals... 48

Permissiveness Blues.. 51

The Baillie 54

Bothy Ballad for a Roustabout.. 56

The Mourners... 58

Thinking of You 62

Oldmeldrum Sports 67

1977

Flora's Letter.. 69

Supermarket.. 71

Jimmy Carter.. 76

The Adjudicator.. 78

We're No Awa' tae Bide Awa'.. 80

The Prize-Giving.. 86

The Return of Bruce and the Spider...................................... 88

1979

The Councillor... 92

The Beechgrove Garden.. 95

Fit D'Ye Ca' 'Im.. 99

The Sleeper...103

It Gets Ye Oot o' the Hoose.. 108

The North-East Oscars...113

The Ashvale...114

Desert Island Discs...117

She's Wonderful...120

1982

The American Visitor...121

Auntie Flo's Tune 124

The A.G.M..126

The Mossat Shop...129

Santa's Phone Call 131

That's Far A' the Money Went 134

This is Your Life 138

Under the Carpet 144

Edinburgh Castle 150

1984

Parents' Night 152

Days Here and There 158

At the Airport 163

Sweet Song 169

The Moderator 170

Ice-Cream 174

Welcome to the World's Bowlers 177

The Hot Line 180

Mounthooly 182

Argyle Street 184

Corstorphine 186

Buying a House 188

Building Societies 193

The Rentokil Man 194

The Bridegroom 197

Musical Family 199

7

1986

The Burns Supper...202

We've No Business...204

Song of the Scottish M.P's...206

The Auchterturra Builder..208

Snooker..214

The Auchterturra By-Election..216

The Auchterturra Band..224

Wedding Guests..228

Younger Than Us..235

At the Assembly 240

Trivial Pursuit...246

The Stop-Go Man...250

Small Hotel...256

The Dinner Dance..258

How Are Things in Auchterturra?...263

Arrival..265

Departure...267

Reputations...270

Foreword

The name of *Scotland the What?* is already well established across the English-speaking world, not least where Scots in exile will gather for a breath of the song and humour of the land they left behind.

For some, records and cassettes are a substitute for the live show they have never been able to see. For others, they are an extension and constant reminder of that exquisite pleasure and an appetiser for the next time they will surrender themselves to the talents of Buff Hardie, Steve Robertson and George Donald.

There was only one dimension of this unique phenomenon which had been missing until now - the printed word. Now we have it in this long-awaited book of song, music and sketch which will delight the faithful and enable a wider audience to gain a whiff of what they have been missing.

If I refer to the 'unique phenomenon' of *Scotland the What?* it is because there is no other way to describe them. Their special brand of comedy is a build-up of character portrayal which culminates in the traditional punch-line. Yet what separates *Scotland the What?* from most other purveyors of comedy I have ever known is that you can hear that punch-line over and over again and find it as funny as the first time.

Indeed one of the problems for this talented team is that their attempts to move on to any new material has often been thwarted by public demand to hear what they know already!

Even those of us who can practically recite, word for word, the invitation to Her Majesty to open the Oldmeldrum Sports or the feats of Sandy Thomson (fower times bowlin' champion o' Auchnagatt) will not be deterred from reliving it all in the printed word and passing it around among less-enlightened friends.

So this book will fulfil a need – and remind us of the remarkable personal story of the *Scotland the What?* team. Meeting first at Aberdeen University, Buff and Steve were writing and performing in students' shows in the 1950s and continued that association in an Aberdeen Revue Group of the 1960s, to which George Donald from Huntly as pianist and composer and James Logan as director were already contributing their own talents.

It was when young families materialised that the quartette decided to ring down the curtain on what had been an absorbing hobby. Where better to make their farewell appearance than the Edinburgh Festival Fringe with a show called for the first time *Scotland the What?* Lo and behold, critics catching up with lost time suddenly discovered this team of Aberdonians and hailed them as the funniest show in town. No, no, this couldn't be the end; just the beginning.

The rest is part of show business history of the last twenty years. They have performed regularly all the way from the home base of His Majesty's in Aberdeen to London's South Bank and gathered up a following which multiplies by the year.

Elsewhere I have described them as 'a modern satirical extension of the mood portrayed by the great Aberdeen comedian, Harry Gordon, with a humour rooted every bit as firmly in their native culture.' More succinctly, they could just be described as 'great entertainers.'

To complicate matters, however, all of them were firmly set in professional careers when show business demanded their full-time attention. They were around the fifty mark when Steve bowed out of his lawyer's practice, George stood down as an assistant rector of Perth Academy, Buff gave up his post as Secretary of Grampian Health Board and scientist James Logan gave up his laboratory to tackle that other chemistry of human talent, in his role as director-manager-agent.

Mirth is now their mission. And as I sit among the converted in many a theatre today, I cannot but reflect on schooldays at Gordon's College, where I was a contemporary of Buff Hardie. The fact that we appeared in a school play together is another story. But I do rather treasure the fact that I witnessed the very first theatrical steps of a future star.

What he and his colleagues have created for our public amusement is now here in glorious print. Let laughter commence.

Jack Webster.

Introduction

'Div ye change the show at a' fan ye ging oot o' Aiberdeen?', asked the Principal of Aberdeen University astutely. It is one of the questions most frequently put to us, and the answer is that we do, though not a lot. We scarcely ever compromise on the dialect (or rather dialects, because there are broadly two, city and country), but we do alter North-East references which would bewilder audiences to whom they are unfamiliar. In all cases the songs and sketches in this book are reproduced as they were performed on home territory, and in case this creates a problem for any non-North-East reader, we would like to offer a few aids to comprehension.

First of all, there is the map. Now, what about this strange place called Auchterturra? There is a bit of dialogue in our current show which may be helpful:

Far is this Auchterturra?
Well, ye ken Methlick?
Aye.
Maud, Torphins, New Pitsligo?
Aye.
Fyvie, Udny, Rhynie, Fogie?
Aye, aye.
Well, it's neen o' them. But it could be ony o' them.

In other words, Auchterturra is our version of the typical Aberdeenshire village.

Secondly, for those readers of a scholarly bent, the text is accompanied by learned footnotes, though we resisted the temptation to explain every reference, partly on aesthetic grounds – a surfeit of footnotes can offend the sensitive eye – but largely because in many cases we couldn't think of anything to say.

However, where there's no footnote and you're still puzzled, you can take it that such a reference was changed to a local one when the show travelled. For example, when *The Baillie* (1975) reached Edinburgh, it was Jenner's doorway which was defiled by the incontinent Celtic supporters. In other words the trick is to look for your own local equivalents. Come to think of it, trick is an apt word, because it has become a necessary trick of our dubious trade to do a bit of sneaky local homework before taking the show anywhere. And this has, incidentally, taught us more about our own country than we ever learned via the Scottish education system.

Of course altering references in this way can be rather hazardous, particularly in the songs, where the performer has virtually no time to adjust a line that is deeply ingrained in the memory. The ultimate example of this was when a whole song changed: *Mounthooly* (1984), itself a parody of Rodgers and Hart's *Manhattan*, became *Argyle Street* in Glasgow and *Corstorphine* in Edinburgh. Happily Union Street never did abut on to the Ubi Chip, nor was there a fly-over from Bearsden to Murrayfield, but some nights it was a close-run thing.

All that said however, there are still some items, though not many, so dense as to defy comprehension by anyone who doesn't belong to the North-East or hasn't a North-East chum. In these cases an (AG) certificate has been granted. Bearing in mind that in the cinema (PG) means parental guidance, the significance of (AG) is that the item is unsuitable for anyone unless accompanied by an Aberdonian (or even better, an Auchterturrian.)

It is one thing understanding references; as to the language, everything will fall into place if you remember that North of Stonehaven wh = f. Thus who, what, where, when become respectively, fa, fit far, fan. As *The Stop/Go Man* (1986) says to the driver of the speeding fire-engine, 'Far's the fire?'

Finally, we assume that readers of this book will almost certainly be Scottish, and will not therefore have the residual problem of the delightful Home Counties lady (a distant relative of one of us) who dutifully came to see the show during a short New Year season in London. Having sat through one of our better nights on which the volume of laughter from the assembled Scottish exiles was, though we say it wirsels, not insignificant, she came round afterwards and greeted her relative with the words, 'How lovely to see you again, and that was obviously a very funny show.'

S.T.W.? 1987

Although male midwives did not become legal until 1979, James Logan acted as one at the birth of *Scotland the What?* in St. Mary's Hall, Albany Street, Edinburgh in August, 1969 during the last week of the Festival Fringe. This picture was taken the night before, when everyone was relaxed and jolly.

L. to R. The young George Donald, the young Buff Hardie and the young Stephen Robertson. (That's James top centre – he was never young.)

In order to be 'with it' and trendy, James looked at M & S sweaters (it was the late sixties), but they ended up in their own dinner suits.

It's been the same ever since, just three men, two chairs and a piano, and a few props, generally hats of one kind or another . . .

. . . except when television required some realistic costumes and settings.

Through the 70's and 80's the show appeared at theatres all over Scotland.

There was a particularly warm welcome in Glasgow, where Steve, always the master of make-up, extended his repertoire by impersonating the Lord Provost.

But home has always been His Majesty's Theatre, Aberdeen . . .

. . . where they met a former customer of the Ballater Toy Shop

. . . having previously met his charming grannie.

But their sternest critics remain their nearest and dearest. Here then is a rare view of the extended *Scotland the What?* family as James conducts a post-mortem following an out-of-town preview.

Hanging on his every word are (L to R) George and **Isabelle Donald**, **Buff** and Margaret Hardie, business manager Graham Hunter, Anne Logan and Steve and Eva Robertson.

The Banker

A man is speaking rather impatiently into an ancient telephone with a separate ear-piece.

Hello-hello-hello. Is that the exchange at Rhynie? Is that you Beldie? Foo ye daein' quine? This is Sandy Thomson spikkin'. Manager o' the Clydesdale Bunk at Auchterturra. Now, Beldie, jist pit awa' yer knittin' for a minutie an' concentrate. 'Cos I'm wintin' ye tae get me a number. Ye hinna done that for a whilie now, have ye? This is a number in Munchen Gladbach. No, no, Beldie, nae Meikle Wartle. Munchen Gladbach, Germany. Munchen Gladbach, funf – nine – double funf. Fit's that Beldie? It's neen o' your business. Ye ill-fashioned besom that ye are. I'm phonin' the bunker there. Mphph. The bunker. No, no, Beldie, nae Hitler's bunker. Hitler's been deid a whilie. Nae the bunker, *the bunker*. Aye, 'cos me an' him's daein' a swap. Something tae dae wi' the Common Market I think it is. But I'm nae richt sure. There was a letter came in aboot it, but the dog swallied it. Aye, well onywye I'm gan ower tae Germany for a whilie. An' the German chiel, he's comin' ower here for a whilie tae rin the bunk at Auchterturra.

Fit's that? Are ye through til him? . . . My God, that's quick! Hello, hello, is that the Bundes – the Bundes . . . can I spik to the manager please? Thank you very much. Hello, is that you Heinrich? Foo are ye? This is Sandy spikkin'. Oh, ye recognised my voice did ye? Weel are ye a' organised? Hiv ye got yer kilt? Good, good. Aye, I've got my leather briks. Weel, I was just giein' ye a phonie, Heinrich, tae see if ye had ony last minute queries aboot Auchterturra, the village and the bunk itsel', like . . . Oh, ye hiv. Uhuh – the size o' Auchterturra? Uhuh – well – I'd put it this wye. As Rhynie is tae Aiberdeen, so is Auchterturra tae Rhynie. The bunk? Computerised? Oh completely computerised. Oh aye, we get a len' o' the addin' machine fae the garage once a month. Mind you, it's awa' bein' sorted iv noo. Aye, a leakage in the paraffin intake pipe. Fit's that? decimalisation? Oh yes, yes, decimalisation has reached Great Britain. And I hope before long it will also reach Auchterturra. Mind you, at the moment, not only is Auchterturra not yet decimalised, Auchterturra is not yet devalued. So one of your main jobbies will be to keep the pound floating as high as you possibly can against the local currency of neeps an' tatties.

Fit's that, Heinrich? Customers? Oh, we've got a pucklie. Weel, there's the laird for a kick-aff. He's yer feudal superior, so always remember to give him a friendly greeting, which in your case, Heinrich, will be a cordial *Seig Heil* and a respectful click o' the heels. Any servile gesture like that goes down a ton wi' the laird, because, as we in the bunk know only too well, his superiority is purely feudal an' nae financial. In fact, he hisna twa bawbees tae rub thegither, an' if he had, he couldna rub them thegither, his hand's that shakky.

That's the laird. Then there's the minister. Ye winna get muckle business oot o' him either. Weel, the manse is crawlin' wi' bairns. Nine o' them he's got – the feel gype. Fan he applied for the job, the Vacancy Committee made a bloomer. They speirt him *his* religion, but they forgot tae ask his wife's.

Then there's Alec Lawrence, the souter. He saw service in the recent war which, at the time, Heinrich, your country was thought to have lost. Alec was wounded at Dunkirk – severely wounded in the thoomb. Eh? No, no, that wis very severe for Alec. Ye need yer thoomb fan yer a souter.

Spikkin' aboot the war reminds me that in 1944 a pucklie German prisoners o' war were sent tae Auchterturra an' they were locked up in Tam Ferguson's barn. Tam's got a Dutch barn – that's the nearest we could get tae mak them feel at hame. Now, I dinna ken ony German mysel but fae the noise ye hear comin' oot o' that barn some nichts. I'm just beginnin' tae jalouse that some o' that prisoners think it's time they were let oot. Could you maybe hae a wordie wi' them an' see?

Fit's that? Far *is* a' the siller in Auchterturra? Weel, I suppose the wealthiest man in the village would be Andy Webster the vet. And that's because he's nae just the vet, he doubles as the doctor. So my advice tae you is – keep fit. But if ye hae tae get him in, ye've naethin' tae worry aboot as lang as the complaint that ye are suffering fae is brucellosis, distemper or hard-pad. Just one word o' war-nin'. Watch him fan he's takin' yer temperature.

Weel, I think that's aboot it noo, Heinrich. Hae ye got yer passport? Good, yes, weel I hope ye won't be bothered with too many formalities when ye reach the border . . . at Kennethmont. Aye, I think that's aboot it noo, Heinrich. Cheery-bye then – Auf Weidershen – Dankeshun – Bye-bye.

Beldie – get aff that line, quine, or I'll get the Gestapo tae ye!

Ill-fashioned besom Cf. vratch *The Hot line*.

Neeps and tatties Evidence that Auchterturra has always belonged to the Keynesian school of economics.

Feudal superior Landed relic: useless, chinless and increasingly penniless.

The souter's thoomb Last finger.

Gestapo P.C. Wilson

Father of the Bride

A gentleman wearing a carnation in his button-hole is embarking on a speech.

Reverend Morrison, friends, members of both families, Linda and Gordon. Now, as father of the bride, I wisna gan tae be allowed tae mak a speech here the day. But I just thocht, somebody's got tae say something efter the best man's last joke. Well, ye saw fit happened. Twa waitresses walked oot, Auntie Mina passed oot, an' the minister made a note o' it in his note-book.

Well, now I'm on my feet, what am I going to say? Well, I'm just going to say – what is uppermost in my mind as I look around this large company. And what is uppermost in my mind as I look around this large company is, this large company is costing me two pounds fifty a head. Yes, I never thocht, when Linda first introduced me to Gordon, that within six short months, I would be standin' up here in the Northern Hotel, three hundred and eighty pounds oot' o' pocket. An' it micht hae been mair. There wis a lot o' folk real huffy at nae bein' asked tae this weddin', ye know. Some of you may have noticed the bride's mother is not in the company today. Well, a' body couldna get! An it's nae every Setterday she gets the chance o' a bittie overtime at the cement works.

Of course, when Jean an' me was married it was durin' the war. And we didn't get a grand expensive reception like this. Oh, no. Her auld man never put his hand in his pooch. And our first love-nest wasn't a brand new, luxurious, Stewartie's bungalow at the Bridge o' Don. Oh, no, no. We just had to move in with your granny, Linda – in Jasmine Terrace. It wisna very satisfactory, the three of us sleepin' in that bed settee. But, there was a war on and it was just one of these temporary arrangements that folk had to put up with. And we won't be there much longer. No, well, you see, we've got to move oot now that granny's gettin married again. Mind you, we're all very sorry that granny's not with us this efterneen. But as she said herself, in her own couthie way, 'I'm nae missin' the wrestlin' for that rubbish.' In any event granny couldn't have made it here to-day, because, as some of you well know, last night at Gordon's stag party she broke her zimmer comin' doon the stair in the Harbour Bar.

The main thing is, the rest of you are all here, so come on, let's enjoy ourselves and mak this a weddin' tae remember. I winna forget it in a hurry. I'll be peyin' for it for years through the Abbey National. But when I see my darling Linda looking so lovely, and so happy, that doesn't bother me one bit. And I look forward to when my other daughters have their weddings – Jill and Sandra and Doreen and Wilma and Marigold and Kathleen and Shirley and the triplets.

Stewartie's bungalow Peak of N.E. yuppie ambition in 1973.

'TRUE LOVE O' MINE'

True Love o' Mine

Oh! I love thy gay and lichtsome air,
True love o' mine.
And I love the wind that blows thy hair,
True love o' mine.
I love thy step – as light as a fairy,
I love thee, only thee, my Mary,
True love o' mine.

Oh! I love thy sweet and winsome face,
True love o' mine.
And I love thy light, beguiling grace,
True love o' mine.
I love thy faintly crooked crannie,
I love thee, only thee, my Annie,
True love o' mine.

Oh! I love to hear thee breathing sighs,
True love o' mine.
And I love the starlight in thine eyes,
True love o' mine.
I love thy laugh – it makes me dizzy,
I love thee, only thee, my Lizzie,
True love o' mine.

Oh! I love to look back at the past,
True love o' mine.
And I pray this joy, this bliss, will last,
True love o' mine.
Oh! may that day assail me never
When I, alone, walk through the heather
And meet the three of you together,
True loves o' mine.

Coal

Two men, Mr. Taylor and Mr. Wallace are seated in front of a fire, warming their hands.

T.   That's a rare burnin' fire that!

W.   Oh, it gives oot a good heat, I will say. *(pause).*

T.   Ye canna beat a fine cheery fire.

W.   That's true. That's true. *(pause)*

T.   Well ye know this, Mr Wallace. Me an' the wife, we wis in a hoose last wik – central heating – oil-fired – small bore – cost them eight hunner an' fifty tae pit it in. Wisna half as cheery as that fire o' yours.

W.   I'll bet it wisna.

T.   It wis not! That's a roaster!

W.   Oh aye, it gies oot a good heat, I will say.

T.   Marvellous! *(pause)*

W.   Ah well, I don't know what the ladies are up to. Through in the kitchen there. Supposed tae be makin' the supper. They'll just be bletherin'.

T.   Aye, just spikkin' aboot naethin' at a'. Tell me Mr. Wallace . . .

W.   Yes?

T.   Is that a Baxi?

W.   Oh aye, we swear by the Baxi. Is it a Baxi you've got?

T.   Oh aye. Och, they're great the Baxies. A' ye dae is, last thing at nicht, ye pile it up wi' dross or English nuts, screw doon yer damper, an' awa' tae yer bed.

W.   And the next morning?

T.   The next mornin' – it's oot . . . usually.

W.   Is it? 'At's a peety, 'at. Far did ye get yer Baxi? Wis it Middler's?

T.   No, no. It wis gan tae be. but naebody telt me Middler's has changed hands. It's Bruce Miller's now, ye know. I went in for a fireplace and came oot wi' a melodeon.

W.   And dae ye like playin' the melodeon, Mr Taylor?

T.   Naw, naw. That wis jist a wee joke.

W.   Oh, I'm sorry.

T.   It's a' richt . . . It's a' richt. *(pause)*

W.   We got oor Baxi fae Scott's. We got 10% aff. Mary's brither's a plasterer there.

T.   Very good. Mary's nae wantin' central heatin', then?

W.   Oh, no. We're stickin' tae the coal fire. It's nae jist that it gies oot a good heat–

Both Though it dis gie oot a good heat.

W. But it's a focal point as weel. It gies ye something tae look at. *(they both stare at the fire. There is a pause.)*

T. Fit kind o' coal's that ye're burnin'? Is it Scotch?

W. Best English. No! As you were. Shilbottle. I took it oot o' the left-hand bunker.

T. Eh?

W. Well, we've twa bunkers, ye see. We use the Shilbottle fan we hiv visitors, and the Best English for wir water.

T. It's good burnin' coal Shilbottle.

W. Oh, it's good burnin'. But it's dirty. Well, ye can see ye get a lot o' soot wi' Shilbottle.

T. Yes, that's true. It is, it's real dirty!

W. Well, but ye canna hae it baith wyes, Mr Taylor. Yer Shilbottle gies oot a good heat, but it's dirty. Yer Best English disna gie oot such a good heat, but it's nae sae dirty.

T. It's nae sae dirty.

W. It's nae sae dirty, an' it's better for yer water.

T. Better for yer water.

W. Better for yer water, an' 'at's the wye we've twa bunkers.

(Mr. Taylor stares at him in disbelief for a few seconds)

T. Foo often div ye get it swept?

W. Fit?

T. Yer chimney.

W. Oh . . . . It's hard tae say.

T. Ah. Fa's yer sweep?

W.	Oh, he's quite a young chap. He's all electric.
T.	Even his bill gies ye a shock. Ha, ha!
W.	No, he's quite reasonable.
T.	Of course, they're all all-electric now. But div you mind the aul' days when he used tae come wi' his lang poles an' pit his brush up the lum?
W.	An' the ballie doon.
T.	And there wis soot a' wye. They've come a lang way since then, the sweeps. It's really wonderful what science can do.
W.	Yes. This is true. If they could jist find a cure for the common cold.
T.	Fa? Sweeps?
W.	Of course, my mither didna believe in sweeps.
T.	Was she an agnostic?
W.	Naw, naw, she jist used tae put a paper up the lum twice a wik. An' ye ken this, in a' the years I kent my mother – Mum never once had a fall of soot.
T.	Very good. Very good. An' her lum never went on fire?
W.	Nuh.
T.	Never?
W.	Nuh.
T.	Not once?
W.	There was eence.
T.	Ah!
W.	An' I can put a date on't. It was the 21st April 1943. It was the nicht o' the big blitz. I could sweer that Germans could see that bleezin' lum a' the wye ower fae Stavanger.

T. We lost a budgie in the big blitz.

W. Oh, I'm sorry.

T. Oh, it's a'richt. It wid hiv been deid by now onywye. Watch! It's spittin'! Watch yersel! that's a bit o' slate.

W. Nae among the Shilbottle! Oh that's shockin', that. Course that's nae the Shilbottle's fault. That's Ellis and McHardy's fault.

T. Well, that's very disappointin', that.

W. That's nae the kind o' thing ye expect fae Ellis and McHardy. That's the kind o' thing ye expect fae the Co-opie.

T. Dinna spik tae me aboot the Co-opie. Nae for coal. We used tae get oor coal fae the Co-opie. A disaster! The coal was aye weet.

W. Aye?

T. I'll tell ye foo weet it wis! We had tae put half the load in the spin drier. Ha, ha!

W. Here, that *is* weet!

T. Well, I'll tell ye this – it didna dae wir sheets ony good.

W. No, I'll bet it didna *(Mr Taylor turns away in exasperation)* Er . . . changin' the subject Mr Taylor . . .

T. Yes?

W. What aboot yer own coal fire, now? Does it give you any trouble in the mornin'?

T. Nae trouble at a'. We just dinna light it! Naw, seriously, a' we dae is, we take last nicht's *Evening Express*, yesterdays *Daily Mirror*, row them up intae paper ballies, a pucklie kindlin', twa Zips, three Drummer Boys, a half gallon of petrol and WHOOSH, it's away!

Twa bunkers In this case the two bunkers *are* bunkers. Cf. *The Banker* where the two bunkers are bankers.

Agnostic Housewife with no faith in chimney sweeps.

Co-opie The Northern Co-operative Society Ltd. abbreviated to (i) Norco, as in Norco House – see *Jimmy Carter*, (ii) the Co-op, pronounced Copie.

The Scottish Plumber

There was a plumber,
A Scottish plumber,
No finer man than he
To mend your W.C..
This prince of plumbers
Could beat all comers,
So quite exclusive was his clientele.

Such wealthy creatures
As bobbies and teachers
Came to depend on him,
They'd always send for him
To mend their toilet;
He widna spoil it.
They knew that he'd do it well.

And so they always got this mister in,
When they'd a blister in –
Side their cistern.
No one ever showed such artistry
In a lavatory as he.

Things for the plumber
Were slack in summer,
But when the winter came
Then things were not so tame;
When it got colder,
A suppie solder
He often had to use on pipes that burst.

The jobs came faster,
And a headmaster
Had a calamity
And, near insanity,
He phoned the plumber,
And told him, 'Come, or
I'll soon be totally submerged.

My plumbing's gone, please clear the drain for me,
Mend the main for me,
Pull the chain for me,
For no one else can avert catastrophe
In my W.C. for me'.

The Newspaper   (AG)

A man is seated at home reading a newspaper clearly visible as the Aberdeen
Evening Express.

Well, what's happenin' in the world the day, then? Eh? 'Mastrick Mums?'
What's the Mastrick mums up to now? 'Mastrick Mums Lash Council In
Bairns Heartbreak Holiday Mix-up Row.' That's jist sensationalism that!
That's irresponsible gutter journalism of the worst order. Just whippin' folk up
intae a frenzy of indignation. Ye can jist see the folk in Fountainhall Road
frothin' at the mou' when they read this! Oh, here's Sheriff Russell dishin' it oot
again. Fa's he pit aff the road the day then? Uh-huh I'm nae surprised; he's
been workin' for that for a whilie. *(turns to back page)* . . .

'Sporting News. Manager Turnbull has injury problem.' Uh-huh. Oh, he's raxed his back pittin' oot the bucket. 'Harry Bannerman wins Open.' ... Oh, it's the Ballater Open. that's jist aboot Harry's stretch this year.

'Births, Marriages and Deaths.' ... Deaths now ... Uh-huh ... Uh-huh ... Nae a death worth a damn ... Oh, as you were, as you were, Peter's away. 'On November 12 at 48b, Union Grove,' the residence of his bidie-in. What aboot the births now ... the births ... 'McDonald. Irene and David are on cloud nine following the safe arrival of Karen Louise, a darling step-sister for Justin.' And fa dis Justin belang til? That's fit I want tae ken. Fit kind o' hippy kibbutz is that for a bairn tae be brocht up in? Marriages now . . . 'Suddenly at King's College Chapel . . . ?

Properties for sale ... Oh, my God ... what a hooses. Here's a photie o' a but an' ben. 'This delightful rural residence, with south-facing back door. Soundly constructed and in need of only minor repairs to the roof, walls and foundations. For Sale, with vacant possession.' Nae wonder it's vacant! 'Just seventy-one miles from Aberdeen on the main B9469½.' Well, that's a blessin'. 'Between Maggienockater and Botriphnie.'

Oh, here we go, 'North-East Estates.' Uh-huh. Fa's leavin' a' the money this wik now? My God! £537,000 gross. Fa's that then? 'Retired monumental mason.' There's been some richt chisellin' gan on there, I'll tell ye. Oh, I beg his pardon, he's left ten quid tae the North Kirk. The Christian gentleman that he is. Oh, and there's Willie Lovie. What did Willie leave? My God, twa thoosand. His aul' man left him forty thoosand jist last December. He's poured the hale lot ower his throat in less than a year. What a wye tae go!

Oh me, adverts . . . adverts. A hale page advert for Kenny's latest chipper. Nae anither Kenny's! He's got mair branches than the Co-opie in its hey-day. Fit's this een sellin' now, eh? Oh, my gosh! 'curries, omelettes, scampi, pizzas.' Fit's a pizza? 'Spare ribs, chicken Maryland.' A'thing but a bag o' chips!

Oh, here we go, 'Monday's Brides.' There's some richt eens here! Oh, ho, see if we can pick oot the bride o' the wik then? Well, it's nae her onywye. Bride o' the wik? Mair like Bride o' Frankenstein. Oh, uh-huh . . . Here! I ken her! It's Lorraine doon the road. Och, I never thocht Lorraine would get a man. Oh Lorraine, ye should have kept yer specs on. She's nae bonnie wi' them on, but she's worse wi' them aff.

Page five, middle page, World News . . . 'Third World War imminent . . . says Councillor Collie.' 'America . . . Watergate . . . Nixon says . . .' Nixon . . . Oh, he should pack it in that bloke. He's a bigger rogue than Varga . . . Uh-huh . . . an' that's it! *(Turning back to the front cover)* Back tae the Mastrick Mums. There's jist naethin' in this paper at a' nooadays.

31

You're the Top

A hymn to Scottish excellence with some assistance from Cole Porter.

You're the top, you're sheer perfection,
You're the top, you're the Burrell Collection,
You're the golfing style of Sandy Lyle at Troon,
You're the one and only Billy Con'lly,
You're Daphne Broon.
You're the top, you're a sweater by Pringle,
You're the top, you're a malt that's single;
I'm a whisky glass that's down to its last few drops,
But baby, if I'm the bottom, you're the tops.

You're the top, you're J.M. Barrie,
You're the top, you're the great Sir Harry,
You're McGona-gill singing of the Sil-v'ry Tay,
You're Skye, you're Arran, you're Bill McLaren,
You're Hogmanay.
You're the air, that fills Glenshee, dear,
You're a share in the T.S.B., dear;
I'm a Wee Free binge where there's nothing but ginger pop,
But, baby, if I'm the bottom you're the top.

You're the top, you're Ben Macdhui,
You're the top, you're a large Drambuie,
You're the kind of fee a Scots Q.C. can earn,
You're the Glesca polis, you're William Wallace,
You're Bannockburn.
You're a rose, you're Charlotte Square,
You're the prose of Norman Mair;
I'm the World Cup Team, just a shattered dream, a flop,
But baby, if I'm the bottom, you're the top.

You're the Spey, you're Glesca patter.
You're a day gan doon the watter,
You're a Trossachs trek that I'd thoroughly rec-ommend,
You're that loveable rascal, Ian McCaskill,
You're the *People's Friend*.
You're the top, you're a Tartan Special,
You're the top, your Edinburgh Cestle;
We three should quit, 'cos we're practic'ly fit to drop.
But, baby, if we're the bottom, you're the top.

'CINEMAS'

Ye citizens of Aberdeen, nae wonder that ye glower. They hae closed anither picter hoose, The Majestic's days are o-wer, Ye canna hold up progress, Ye canna stop the bingo, So a' the picter hooses are banished in-to lim bo. Lim—bo, lim—bo, they're banished in-to lim-bo

Soon we'll reach the bitter end of all our pic—ture hoo——ses.

34

Cinemas

Ye citizens of Aberdeen,
Nae wonder that ye glower.
They hae closed anither picter hoose,
The Majestic's days are ower.
Ye canna hold up progress,
Ye canna stop the bingo,
So a' the picter hooses
Are banished into limbo.
Limbo, limbo, they're banished into limbo.

I mind ae day in childhood
I wis readin' o' my *Beano*,
When faither came and telt me,
'Son, they're closin' the Casino.'
So fell the old Casino
Where aye there was the danger
Ye wid ging in wi' a freen', but
Ye wid come oot wi' a stranger.
A stranger, a stranger, ye wid come oot wi' a stranger.

Time passed, I stopped *The Beano*,
Started Woodbines, switched tae Players,
And to coortin' at the picters
In the back row up the stairs.
I wis kissin' Jeannie Campbell,
And – who would have supposed it?
We got locked inside the Astoria
When someone went and closed it.
Closed it, closed it, when someone went and closed it.

The City and the Kingsway,
The Cinema Hoose and Gaumont;
How many years of magic
Are snuffed out in one brief moment?
Each year another closes,
One by one the list reduces,
Very soon we'll reach the bitter end
Of all our picture hooses.

Stranger A flech. The entymological connotation is confirmed in the quotation from *Teach Yourself Entymology* in *Bruce and the Spider* (q.v.), which, if continued would read, 'slaters, snails, slugs, spiders, strangers.'

35

Bruce and the Spider

A creature with two waving antennae, is seated centre stage almost concealed by a copy of The Scotsman *it is reading. The front page banner headline proclaims:* ENGLISH ADVANCE. WILL BRUCE SURRENDER? *The newspaper is lowered and we find the creature is a spider.*

S.   Land o' the shining river. Land o' my high endeavour. Land o' my heart forever. Scotland... Oh, yer oot o' the game! The English has over-run the borders. The lecherous soldiery is lootin', an pillagin' an' ravishin' an'... Oh, an' a' thing. But fit can I dae aboot it? A mere spider. Fit am I onywye? I'm nae an insect. I'm nae a mammal. I'm nae a marsupial – I've nae pooches. I'm nae a bird. I'm nae a reptile. I'm nae even a bloomin' fish. Fit am I? I'll tell ye fit I am 'cos I've got it in my little book here. (He produces a tiny book) In fact that's a big book fan yer a spider. *Teach Yourself Entymology.* Spiders now, spiders?... snails... slugs... slaters... centipedes... spiders – here we go! Right!... Oh me! I'm an arachnid, I've got a cephalothorax, I've got twa spinarets, I've got fower pairs o' walkin' legs, an' a – Oh – that's nae nice that. I've got a non-segmented abdomen. Oh fit a sotter.

(Enter Robert the Bruce, wearing a crown and carrying a sword)

B.   A cave, a cave, a refuge, a haven, a harbour, a port, a cave, a cave.

S.   Oh my God, it's big Iain Cuthbertson!

B.   What creepy crawly, hell-sent beast is this?

S.   Hello.

B.   Ye Gods! the monster spiks! What are ye?

S.   I'm a spider.

B.   Ye mean ye're an arachnid wi' a cephalothorax and a non-segmented abdomen?

S.   Here! You seem tae ken a' aboot me? Fit aboot you. Who are you?

B.   I am but a traveller.

S.   A traveller? D'ye like yer job? Here, I think I've got a' thing I'm wantin' the day. Oh no, wait a minutie, wait a minutie. Have ye got ony o' that sticky fly-paper? 'Cos I jist canna catch flies at a'. They come buzzin' doon aboot my heid an' I just canna catch them at a'. I feel thwarted. I've lost he'rt. I'm a frustrated spider.

B. Na, na. I'm nae a commercial traveller. I am your *king*.

S. Oh, pull the other seven.

B. I tell you I am your king. Robert the Bruce.

S. Oh, sire, Good my liege. Custodian o' Scotia's shores. Scottish soldier o' soldiers. Would you like a drink?

B. Na, na. I hinna time. I hinna time. The English are at my heels.

S. Oh. *(He gives a puzzled glance round the back of Bruce's feet)*

B. Wheesht!

S. I'm wheeshtin'.

B. What was that? . . . Ah, it's but the rain.

S. Oh! Oh is't rainin'? Oh me, that means somebody's squashed een o' my chums.

B. I maun flee. I maun reach Skye the nicht.

S. Skye, Skye, oh aye. You've tae meet Flora, hiv ye? . . . Oh no, you're nae that een.

B. Na, it's your king you see. But an unworthy king. Driven into shameful flight by an awesome foe. Proud Edward of England.

S. Oh, but ye can easy beat him! he's just a big Nancy.

B. I've done my best tae avenge the bleed o' Wallace.

S. Wallace? Willie Wallace? Oh, I kent him fine. He was quartered here. And then he went doon tae London and he was quartered there. Oh they tell me he hung aboot there for a whilie.

B. Now I can dee nae mair. I'm finished and Scotland wi' me. My sodgers are slain, the crops are levelled, The towns destroyed. An' I've an affa headache.

S. Oh but we'll soon cure that now Robert. Just a couple o' aspirins. Take aff that weet armour an' awa' tae yer bed. And afore ye go now, ye'll hae a drink?

B. I will, thanks.

S. *(Producing two very small goblets)* Onything ye like, as lang as it's sherry. 'Cos that's a' I've got.

B. Sherry would be fine. Sherry's grand.

S. Dry Fly?

B. Well, here's all the best.

S. An' the same to you, an' a happy New Year when it comes.

B. Lang may yer lum reek.

S. We're no awa' tae bide awa'.

B. Here's tae us.

S. Wha's like us? Damn few, an they're a' deid.

B. Deid!

S. Aye, deid.

B. An' deid is what they will be! The flooers o' the forest cut doon in their prime. What am I to do?

S. Well dinna get sae workit up aboot it, Robert. A man o' your age. I'll tell ye fit tae dee. A' ye hiv tae dee is *(He whispers in Bruce's ear).*

B. He's right! Try, try, try again. It's taken a spider tae show me the wye. Try, try, try again! Tae victory! *(Bruce exits brandishing his sword)*

S. Robert, Robert, Robert, Robert . . . Oh me, he's nae wise that king. I didna say, 'Try, try, try again.' I said 'Try Dry Fly again.'

Iain Cuthbertson Winner of BAFTA Best Actor Award for *The Wallace* (1295)

The Will

Mr. Hunter, a solicitor is seated at a table. Mr. Christie, a client, appears at the door.

H. Sit you down Mr. Christie

C. Thank you, sir.

H. Nice to see you.

C. To see you nice.

H. Well now, you've come in to make your will?

C. Aye.

H. Well, that's very sensible.

C. God! I'm nae lookin' as bad as that, am I?

H. Not at all, on the contrary, you're looking very well for a man of your age. How old are you?

C. Ah now . . .

H. I would put you at about mid-sixties?

C. Na.

H. Seventy?

C. Na.

H. Seventy-five?

C. Gettin' warmer.

H. Eighty?

C. Chappin'.

H. Well that's very good.

C. Excuse me for askin' ye . . .

H. Yes, you just ask any question you like.

C. Can I take aff my bonnet?

H. Well, I wouldn't bother. This shouldn't take us a minute. Let's begin at the beginning.

C. Weel noo, I jist thocht it wis time I wis gettin' my affairs in order, 'cos I'm gan awa' on my holidays. I'm gan awa' tae see my brither. I hinna seen my brither for – oh – forty year . . .

H. Forty years, Good heavens! And where did your brother go off to?

C. Oh, doon aboot Fettercairn.

H. Now the first thing we've got to establish is what you've got to leave.

C. Weel, I'm gan tae leave my Playboy calendars tae the minister, my bowls and my walkin' stick tae the ladies o' the guild . . .

H. Yes, yes, but what about your main assets?

C. No complaints at a'. Nae since I hid the operation five year syne.

H. Prostate?

C. Oh, flat oot.

H. Well, well. Now, what about your heritable property? You own your own farm?

C. Oh aye, Sharnydubs o' Boghillock o' Bourtie Brae . . . Mains.

H. Now, you would have an acre or two at Sharnydubs?

C. Oh aye, a fair bit o grun'! But it's affa rough ye see. An' then doon the howe yonder, ye ken, far the polluted burn meets the road, that's the road that gets blocked wi' sna' – every August – it's naethin' but bog. It's a helluva place Sharnydubs. It couldna be worth mair nor – oh – three or four hunner thoosand. Maybe five hunner thoosand at a pinch.

H. Excuse me, I think you could maybe take your cap off.

C. Thank you very much *(He takes his cap off)*.

H. Well now, it certainly sounds as if you've got something to leave.

C.   And I jist want tae be fair tae a' body.

H.   Well, what about beneficiaries? Is there a Mrs. Christie?

C.   Aye, aye is there. There is a Mrs. Christie. An' my main concern is this. Fit wye can we cut the auld besom oot?

H.   Well you see, we can't cut her out entirely.

C.   Can we nae? Can I nae dae fit I like wi' my money? Ye ca' that justice?

H.   Well, Mr. Christie, I don't deal with justice, I deal with the Law of Scotland. And as your widow, she is entitled to one third of your moveable estate. That's everything you've got in the bank.

C.   Oh na, na, I dinna believe in the bunk, no, no.

H.   Nothing in the bank?

C.   Well, I did hae an overdraft, but I withdrew't.

H.   Well, do you keep cash at home, in a safe maybe?

C.   Na, na, I dinna believe in a safe either, no, no. I've got a biscuit tin though. Does that coont noo? Aneath the bed, ye ken. Jist aside the . . .

H.   Yes, a biscuit tin would count. How much money would you have in the biscuit tin?

C.   Oh maybe seventy, eichty . . .

H.   Seventy or eighty pounds?

C.   Thoosand. Seventy or eichty thoosand, Mphph.

H.   But that's a lot of money!

C.   Div ye think that noo?

H.   Well to keep in a biscuit tin.

C.   Oh aye, but I ta'en the biscuits oot first.

H.   Yes, yes, but you see seventy or eighty thousand pounds in a biscuit tin . . . you're not getting any interest on that.

41

C. Aye, that's richt, nae interest . . . an' nae tax.

H. Well now, how about the rest of your family? Are there any children?

C. Aye, there's my daughter, Ina, but dinna bother aboot Ina, we've seen Ina a'richt. Fit a rare send-off we gied her, a rare weddin' at King's College Chapel, and then on tae the Station Hotel . . . Rhynie. Fit a rare day. A'body was fou'. An' that was at King's College Chapel afore we *got* tae the Station Hotel, Rhynie.

H. Is there a station at Rhynie?

C. No, but they were aye hopin'.

H. Well, if you're cutting out your daughter as well, who *are* you leaving your money to?

C. Well, there's this lady in Union Grove.

H. Oh, yes!

C. My niece.

H. Oh, yes! Could I have her name?

C. You could not. You find yer ain niece. It took me lang eneuch before my charm did the trick.

H. Well, but you see, if she's a beneficiary, I've got to have her name.

C. Is that richt noo, is that the law? Weel I'll write it down for ye. *(He takes a pencil and pad from Mr. Hunter and begins to write)*

H. Well, whoever she is, she's a very lucky lady.

C. Ah weel, but she's made me a very happy man . . . twice a wik this last twinty year.

H. Twice a week?

C. Aye, Wednesday . . .

H. Wednesday and . . .

C. Oh, jist Wednesday. Twice ilka Wednesday. *(He returns the pad on which he has written the name)*.

H. Well, well . . . Good grief, that's my Auntie Madge!

C. Oh well, my loon, in the end o' the day the biscuit tin'll maybe come to you.

Chappin' To chap (v. intr.): to rap on the table with one's knuckles, thus indicating to one's opponents that ye're missin' yer shottie

'OUR GLENS'

With a strong feeling of pride

I love Scot-land's glens_____, and what-ev-er else we lose_____, Please leave us our glens_____, Our glo-ri-ous glens_____, our

Our Glens

I love Scotland's glens,
And whatever else we lose,
Please leave us our glens,
Our glorious glens.

Our mountains are grand –
Ben Lomond, Ben Nevis too.
You can have all these bens,
But leave us our glens.
Glenfiddich, Glenlivet, Glendronnach, Glen Grant,
Can you do without them? If you must know I can't.
Put a drop in a glass of Glen Spey or Glendrottar –
It's a perfectly bearable way to drink water.

I'd willingly lose
Our culture or most of it,
For instance that mess
Called 'Full Highland dress.'
With the whole ethnic bit,
With haggis and Hogmanay,
I'd gladly dispense,
But leave us our glens.
Glenfarclas, Glenlochy, Glengarioch, Glenfaul,
I once knew a man who had sampled them all.
Glenugie, Glenkinchie, Glenisla, – that's plenty,
He looked sixty-five but in fact he was twenty.

Take our Highland schottische,
Our marches, strathspeys and reels,
Take our old Scottish waltz,
But leave us our malts.
Remove, if you will,
Our ladies' conveniences
And our gentlemen's,
But leave us our glens.
Glenturret, Glen Scotia and last week Glen Fyne
Was rare at Communion when they ran out of wine.
Glenglassough, Glenlossie, Glendullan, Glenmorangie,
I prefer them to Cointreau, which I find too orangie.

Oh! breathes there a Scot
Whose views on priorities,
When laid on the line,
Are different from mine?
Take our jobs, take our homes,
Take anything else you will –
Wife, family and friends –
But leave us our glens.

Hospitals

Two men, Mr Black and Mr Sangster are standing at a bar each with a pint glass in hand.

S.   Did ye hear aboot Arthur?

B.   No.

S.   Arthur's in hospital.

B.   Oh, far aboot?

S.   Foresterhill.

B.   Oh.

S.   His ain docter could make naethin' o' him. So he pit him tae Woolmanhill.

B.   Oh.

S.   And they pit him tae the City Hospital for his he'rt.

B.   Oh.

S.   An' he'd a' the tests o' the day. But it wisna his he'rt.

B.   Oh.

S.   So they pit him tae Woodend.

B.   Oh – Glenburn?

S.   No, Woodend.

B.   An' fit did they say?

S.   They said he was ill.

B.   Oh.

S.   But their tests never showed naethin'

B.   Never showed naethin'.

S. No.

B. Oh.

S. Aye, then he was oot at Kingseat for a coupla days.

B. Oh.

S. Well, he enjoyed it fine.

B. Kingseat?

S. Aye.

B. 'At's the place for folk that get depressed.

S. 'At's richt, weel he did. He did get affa depressed efter a while. So then they ta'en him in as a last resort, tae Foresterhill.

B. Oh.

S. An' that's far he is noo.

B. Oh.

S. An' he's had a' the tests o' the day. He's had bleed tests. He's had urine tests. *(Balefully Mr Black looks into his glass)* He's had tubes. He's had a thing in his airm. He's had a thing up his nose.

B. But Arthur aye had a thing up his nose. *(Mr B. indicates inside his own nose)* Tell me, has he had X-rays?

S. Aye, an' they never did him nae good either. An' he's had a' the specialists o' the day roon' aboot his bed. An' ye ken fit they've come up wi'?

B. No.

S. They've come up wi' his liver.

B. Oh.

S. They say he's got St. Cyrus.

B. Naw, naw, nae St. Cyrus ... Cirrhosis.

S. Oh, cirrhosis. Fit dis cirrhosis mean?

B. Well, that means he taks a helluva bucket.

S. Well, I coulda telt them that.

St. Cyrus Disease of the liver near Montrose

Permissiveness Blues

I get a thrill just thinkin' I live in Aberdeen
Where couples all are swoppin' – it's just one big swingin' scene.
There's swingin' and there's swoppin' for all to see
There's thousands that I fancy, but they won't swing with me.
I get no chance to practise my views.
I got the hearin'-about-the-action, but gettin' no satisfaction
Permissiveness blues.

I once was at a party, where couples came to swing
And all the fellers' car keys were tossed into the ring.
But whoever got mine did not admit that she had.
I had to walk home and the weather was bad.
A car key is a bad thing to lose.
I had the feelin'-very-angry, hoofin'-it-home-from-Banch'ry
Permissiveness blues.

My secret'ry, Mrs. Williams, she lives near Peterhead.
I fancied swinging with her. 'Let's get together,' I said.
But when I suggested her place, she said, 'Do you mind?'
She told me she was Brethren – of the very close kind.
Driving her home, I had to try to defuse.
I had the all-aboard-for-Sodom, but-ended-up-in-Boddam
Permissiveness blues.

At last I met a couple who lived in a high rise flat.
I'd heard that they would swing at the drop of anyone's hat.
They came round for an evenin' of swingin' sin,
But when they saw my missus, they packed the whole thing in.
A glimps of Babs, and they made their adieus;
I had the very-nearly-made-it, but once-again-frustrated
Permissiveness blues.
  We got the nobody-will-swing-with-us,
  Have a swoppy-fling-with-us
  Do their permissive-thing-with-us blues.
  We got the nobody-stays-long-with-us
  Nobody-goes-strong-with-us
  What-the-hell-is-wrong-with-us blues.
  We got the blues.

Permissiveness The Swingin' Sixties reached Aberdeen late, and *Scotland the What?* even later, half-way through the Seventies.

'PERMISSIVENESS BLUES'

With abandon, ♩ = 104

I get a thrill just thinkin'_____ I live in Aber——deen_____ Where couples all—— are swop-pin'; ____ it's just one big swing—ing scene____ There's swingin' & there's swoppin' for all to see There's thousands that I fancy but they won't swing with me. I get no chance to practise my views. I got the hearin' a-bout the ac-tion, but gettin' no sa-tis-fac-tion

The Baillie

Usher: Court . . . Court will be upstanding for your presiding magistrate today, Councillor Alexander Swick.

(A red-gowned Baillie enters and seats himself on the bench. He checks his watch and looks around.)

Baillie: Right, 2.30, time for the first race – the first case. Right, Mr. Physical – bring in the first criminal. Eh, eh, fit's that? Fit's that Mr Physical? Innocent till proved guilty? Fa's side are you on? A'right, a'right, I take the point, I take the point. Bring in the hooligan onywye. Right, stand up there, Jim. An' tak' that smile aff yer face fan I'm spikkin' tae ye. An' fit wye are ye nae handcuffed? Oh, you're the solicitor! Look, I'm nae carin' fa ye are, I'm in charge here. O.K.? Now watch it, sweetheart, watch it. Fit's yer name onywye? You're new! Far's Frunkie Lefevre the day? Oh, he's a great Frunkie, is he? He's a great Frunkie! Frunkie selt my hoose for me. Took a bit o' daein', it was a cooncil hoose.

Right, this is your client is't? A nesty lookin' bit o' work, I must say. Right, far's the charge sheet? Oh ho ho ho, they've fairly thrown the book at you, boy. Oh ho ho ho, baith sides. I've never seen that afore. Very good, very good! Eyes down for the first charge. Listen now! This is important tae you. Maks nae odds tae me. I'm gan hame for my tea efter this.

Right, now, the first charge is, that on November fourteenth, in Union Street, you did make an unprovoked assault on twelve defenceless Celtic supporters, and that while doing so, you did indulge in verbal abuse of a sectarian nature, relating indelicately to the person of his Holiness the Pope. Fit exactly did ye say? Oh, for ony sake. Now, I take a very serious view of this offence, being a left-footer mysel' – in the footballing sense only, of course. I mean, these twelve Celtic supporters, welcome visitors to our city, were entitled to its traditional courtesy. There they were, honoured ambassadors of sport, nae hermin' naebody, quietly urinating in E & M's doorway, when you cam' up an' pit the heid in. This court will never condone violence of any kind. If it wis up tae me, you would get the birch.

Now the second charge is of an even more serious nature, and it is that on November seventeenth, you did inscribe graffiti on a jetty at Fittie. Now, that's a pity. But we canna hae this kind o' thing in the city. I mean, this graffiti is spreading a' wye. In St. Nicholas Hoose, in the lord Provost's private bog – cloakroom, the wa's is covered wi't. Jist the other day, I saw Robbie Lennox, wi' his aerosol can in his hand, skitin' up on the wa' 'Sandy Mutch is a big fat neep.' Well, it's childish that, is it? Childish.

Now, in this case I do not propose to call any evidence, 'cos it just gets me a'

mixed up. Well, this isnae an easy job. I ken fit you're thinkin'. You're thinkin ony feel could dae't. Well this is one feel that canna. Now, prisoner at the bar, before I pass sentence, how do you plead? Guilty or not guilty? . . . Not Proven? You plead Not Proven? We've never had that afore! That's very clever that. But ye winna mak a monkey oot o' me, Jim. Because this is the District Court, where justice has not only to be done, it has to be seen to be believed.

Mr Physical Official designation of the public prosecutor in the Aberdeen legal system.

Frunkie Lefevre M.A., Ll.B. A well-known Aberdeen hotelier and racing driver.

Bothy Ballad for a Roustabout

Tune: *The Pawky Duke*

There eence wis a very orra loon
Ca'd Lubin John McRafferty.
He lived alane in a but an' ben
At Mains o' Tilliescatterty.
Now Lubin Jock the local folk
Swore 'Guid Almichty God, O!
He's daft as a brush, wi' the brains o' a thrush
An' he looks like Quasimodo'.
But for a' that Jock wis a real dumb cluck –
Nae gumption, sense or guile –
Even Jock could see wi' half a glae e'e
There wis siller in North Sea ile.
       Jock's nae an orra man the day,
       And it's a' because o' North Sea ile.

Jock went alang tae a roughneck gang
Far the lads a' looked like Samson.
He got kitted oot in a biler suit,
But he kept his Nicky Tams on.
Helicopter flight got Jock uptight,
'Cos hichts he couldna maister;
At the Turra Show he'd got vertigo
Climbin' on tae a combine hairster.
The chopper ae day began tae sway –
A maist alarmin' motion.
Jock's he'rt aboot stopped and the feel gype dropped
His piece intae the ocean.
       Jock's nae an orra man the day,
       And it's a' because o' North Sea ile.

At the end o' a tour Jock came ashore
Wi' his wallet full nae handy.
He thocht he wid speed tae Peterheid
For a touch o' the hoochmagandy.
Six exports, syne he met a quine,
Says she, 'Can I be of service?
I'm a high class quine, 'cos I've served my time
At Mintlaw and St. Fergus.
I'm a *fille de joie*, and I chauve awa'
And I think that I dae my work well.
It's maybe nae fair, but I'm makin' much mair

Than I did wi' Crosse an' Blackwell.'
>Jock's nae an orra man the day,
>And it's a' because o' North Sea ile.

Says the sonsie lass, 'Ye've tae pey in cash –
In Sterling, gold or dollars.
For anither 10p plus V.A.T.
I micht jist tak oot my rollers.'
Well, Jock an' the quine had sic a good time
Fulfillin' each other's yearnin's
It occurs tae John they could baith live on
Her ile-related earnin's.
Next week they got spliced; says Jock, 'That's nice.
My workin' days is over.
She'll mak a pile aff the lads in the ile,
And I will be in clover.'
>Jock's wife has set him up for life,
>A' because o' North Sea ile.

Orra loon Farm worker, so-called because he has a powerful charisma about him.

Nicky Tams Dalyell's boxer shorts.

Hoochmagandy Cry of Hindu pacifist during eightsome reel.

Chauve awa' To build a dyke laboriously.

Crosse and Blackwell Clearly at an early stage in her career the *fille de joie* had been a can-can girl.

The Mourners

A Mr. Bruce is discovered seated in a crematorium with a hymn book on his knee. There is another hymn book on the empty chair beside him. The organist is playing Sheep May Safely Graze. *Mr Bruce waves cheerily to friends whom he notices elsewhere in the crematorium. Enter Mr. Simpson who taps him on the shoulder. Mr Bruce responds to his unspoken enquiry and ushers him into the vacant seat. Mr. Simpson sits on the hymn book and rises again with a little squeak. They exchange smiles as Mr. Simpson sits down again. Both put their hymn books on their laps and simultaneously compose their features into a semblance of sorrow.*

S. It must have been very sudden.

B. At the end.

S. I didna ken he was ill.

B. He wasna ill ... naethin' serious onywye. No, no, the day afore his eighty-third birthday, he cam doon the stairs in the mornin', took in the milk, put the kettle on, an' he was away.

S. I didna see it in the paper. He's lucky I'm here.

B. It wasna in the paper.

S. Aye wis it. The wife telt me. It wis in the country edition o' the Green Final.

B. I went tae Kaimhill by mistake. I didna ken aboot this new place.

S. Oh aye, it's been on the go a whilie. I wis at a funeral here last wik. Only it wis next door in Cinema 2.

(without moving his body, Mr. Bruce looks behind him, first to the right, then to the left)

B. I thocht Jimmy Watson would've been here. Willie was aye very good tae him.

S. Aye wis he. Is Jimmy Watson nae here? *(not trusting Mr. Bruce's testimony as to Jimmy Watson's absence, Mr. Simpson repeats Mr. Bruce's two movements).* That's Jimmy Watson in the back row ...

(Mr. Bruce looks quickly behind once again)

B. No, that's nae Jimmy Watson. Jimmy Watson's got a hearing aid. An' he hisna got a black tie.

S. Well, it's affa like Jimmy Watson *(Longish Pause)* Wis ye at the match on Setterday?

B. Aye, it was very good. Willie wid've enjoyed it.

S. No he widna. Willie didna like fitba'.

B. He did. He had a season ticket at Pittodrie for thirty year.

S. Oh aye, just so he could get oot the hoose on a Setterday efterneen.

B. I thocht there wid hae been mair folk. *(He makes a count of all those present both in front and behind)* It's nae a great turn-oot. I thocht some o' the boys fae the golf club wid hae been here.

S. No, it's the Wednesday medal the day.

B. An' fit aboot the lads fae Willie's coffee school, are they nae here?

S. No, they couldna come either. Nae fan they heard the service was at eleven o'clock. An' then his son's nae here either . . . Brian.

B. Is Brian nae here? That's funny. I wis spikkin' tae Brian yesterday, an' I wis tellin' him it wis his aul' man's funeral the day, an' he wis certainly intendin' comin'.

S. Ah, weel but he's got affa awkward shifts.

B. Oh that's understandable. But I canna get ower Jimmy Watson nae bein' here.

S. Is that nae Jimmy Watson ower there?

B. Far?

S. Oh, no that's Sandy Lovie fae Auchnagatt. I hinna seen Sandy Lovie fae Auchnagatt since Willie's faither's funeral. The first Hogmanay efter the war.

B. That wis a rare funeral that, wisn't. Fit een's Sandy?

S. He's ower the passage there, twa rows in front on the left hand side. He's got on a black coat, he's got a white mouser, an' he's hair growin' oot his lugs. He must be ninety if he's a day, aul' Sandy. I thocht he wis deid.

B. I think he is deid . . . He's nae movin'.

S. Aye is he. He's chawin' at somethin'.

B. Are you gan back tae the hoose efter this for the biled ham?

S. No, you're nae are ye?

B. Aye.

S. Of course, your Gladys an' Joyce wis very close.

B. Oh aye. Well me an' Gladys an' Joyce an' Willie – the four o' us played whist every Tuesday night for twenty year.

S. Weel, ye'll just need tae play rummy noo. Did your Gladys send flooers?

B. No, did Jessie?

S. No, weel it didna say nae flooers in the paper, ken? But we just thocht he wisna really a floory person.

B. Naw, that's right. Even though he wis a master baker. *(They laugh and control themselves with difficulty)*

60

S. He didna get affa lang tae enjoy his retirement did he?

B. He did! He retired in 1953. He didna dae a hand's turn efter that. Mind you, he didna dae a hand's turn afore that. So it was a bit difficult tae tell fan he did retire.

S. Well, fair play, fair play. Willie cam through the war, ye ken.

S. Oh, but we a' cam through the war, ye ken.

B. Aye, but Willie was wi' the Chindits in Burma.

S. Oh, but I was wi' the REME in Aldershot. An' I'm nae makin' a song an' dance aboot it. There was a bomb fell on oor NAFFI. A doodlebug in fact. The Chindits was never bothered wi' doodlebugs.

B. Here, it must be a real organist the day.

S. Aye, the last time I was here it was records. It was like *The Jimmy Young show.*

B. Fa'll they get for a minister the day? Willie never went tae the kirk.

S. He did!

B. He did not!

S. He did so, Willie was wi' Jimmy Watson an' me at Causeyend Kirk in the 42nd B.B.

B. Oh, aye, sixty year ago.

S. It still coonts.

B. No! I dinna think so.

S. It dis! *(Longish Pause)* Here I ken fit wye Jimmy Watson's nae here!

B. Fit wye?

S. It was his funeral I was here at last wik.

Mouser Large Tash (see *Flora's Letter*)

Jimmy Young Show Funereal radio programme

'THINKING OF YOU'

♩ = 72 Forlornly

Things ap-peared to be   So   right for you and me   Till you met that sche-mer with the
since you went a—way,   All hours   of the day   You are in my thoughts no matter

colla voce

cream Mer—ced—es   You be-came his bride, and you re————side now in   Miln—
what I'm do—ing   wal-king eat-ing drinking, I am   think-ing o-bout

—gavie —————————————. and   you

Walk-ing round the shops, I'm thinking of you——————, Watching Top of the Pops,   I'm

think ing of you_____ I go to Bil—ly Connolly, In a crowded house I'm lonely, Tho' it's

LAST TIME TO CODA

bril—liant, baw-dy and blue_____ I'm thinking of you_____

I'm

in the Alb-any bar with a blonde called Re-né, And af—ter half an hour she's on her

fourth Mar—ti—ni____, But I can't plan the next thing to do, 'cos I

Thinking of You

Things appeared to be
So right for you and me
Till you met that schemer
With the cream Mer-
Cedes.
You became his bride,
And you reside
Now in Milngavie.
And since you went away,
All hours of the day
You are in my thoughts
No matter what I'm doing,
Walking, eating, drinking,
I am thinking
About you.

Walking round the shops,
I'm thinking of you.
Watching *Top of the Pops*,
I'm thinking of you.
I go to Billy Conn'lly,
In a crowded house I'm lonely;
Though it's brilliant, bawdy and blue,
I'm thinking of you.

Painting the garage,
I'm thinking of you.
At Portobello, sur la plage,
I'm thinking of you.
There's a lassie in a teenie
Mr Beaujangles bikini;
Though there's an awful lot in view,
I'm thinking of you.

I'm in the Albany bar
With a blonde called Rene,
And after half an hour
She's on her fourth Martini,
But I can't plan the next thing to do,
'Cos I can't forget about you.

At Murrayfield
I'm thinking of you:
As the Scottish forwards yield,
I'm thinking of you,
And then, as Andy Irvine
Sends an easy goal kick swervin'
Past the post from the 22,
I'm thinking of you.

At the Royal Highland Show
I'm thinking of you.
At the S.N.O.
I'm thinking of you.
They're cheering Ashkenazy,
And it isn't that I'm blasé,
So why don't I cheer too?
I'm thinking of you.

I get myself enrolled
At Jordanhill College,
To divert myself
In a search for knowledge,
But whatever diversion I find,
I can't get you out of my mind.

When *Sportscene* is on,
I'm thinking of you.
My concentration's gone,
I'm thinking of you.
No matter who's been playing,
I'm not hearing what they're saying;
If Archie MacPherson's hair turned blue,
I'd be thinking of you.

Driving round Tollcross,
I'm thinking of you.
I crash the car because
I'm thinking of you.
In the Sheriff's estimation
It's a feeble explanation,
And in Barlinnie, where I am noo,
I'm thinking of you.

Andy Irvine Scottish Rugby full-back. His most recent successor, Gavin Hastings, has been known to miss even more easy goal kicks, but is more difficult to find a rhyme for.

Oldmeldrum Sports

A man is dialling a number on the telephone.

Fower-wan-siven-fower-three-fower-three-five-wan. God, it's a great affair this S.T.V. intit! Hel-hel-hello. Hello, is that Buckingham Palace? Who's spikkin' please? Oh, very nice. Is yer mummy in? Good, can she come tae the phone a minutie? Oh, she's hooverin', is she? I wondered fit that noise wis. I thocht she wis maybe haein' a fly-past . . . A fly-past. No, no, nae her fly. She wid hiv had her fly a whilie ago, it's near denner time. Well, can ye get her tae come tae the phone a minutie? Thank you, mphph. God, he's a richt weel spoken loon that!

Hello-hello-hello-hello? Is that you, yer Majesty? Foo are ye? I wis just giein' ye a phonie – tae see if ye could come and open the Oldmeldrum Sports a wik on Setterday. We had Jimmy Spankie last year. An' we had John Mearns the year afore. An' the committee wis affa keen tae keep up the standard. So you wis the unanimous choice. Jist aboot. Eh? fit's that now? Oh I'm sorry, this is Sandy Thomson, the convenor spikkin'. Aye, I used tae be the bunker at Auchterturra near Rhynie. No, no, the bunker! No, naethin' tae dae wi' golf yer Majesty. No, no, nae the bunker, the *bunker*! That wis till I got the sack. Aye. Fit for? Oh, eh, keepin' futrets in the night safe.

Oh yes, you and I have met though. Oh yes. You maybe winna mind me, though. . . But I mind you. It wis 1954, August the tenth. Does that help ye? No? Ballater Station – guard o' honour – Fourth-seventh Gordon Highlanders. I wis second fae the left in the middle row. In atween Colour Sergeant McLeod and Sandy Webster. Ye dinna mind me? An' ye dinna mind Colour Sergeant McLeod? Oh, but ye div mind Sandy Webster . . . Oh Sandy's fine, yes. Oh, bothered files wi' his lumbago, ken, but nae bad. Fit? Yes, he's still the Station-master at Cambus o' May. Fit's that? Oh weel, naebody never telt Sandy aboot it bein' closed doon . . .

Weel, fit aboot it, quine? 'At's a wik on Setterday at half past two. Now, have ye a diary? Have ye got it handy? Have ye onything on that day? Oh ye hiv! Fit have ye on now? State visit o' the Sheikh o' Abadabi. Ach, jist bring him wi' ye . . . Oh. He has a wife has he? Och, jist bring her an a'. Oh, twenty-fower o' them! Och weel, jist bring the hale jing-bang. An' we'll pit them a' on a float in the pageant . . . Eh? Oh no, no, ye winna hae tae pey. Niver, niver, niver, ma dear. We'll gie ye a complimentary ticket. An' half price for the bairns.

Now, could ye tak somethin' wi ye for the bring an' buy? Fit'll ye tak wi' ye now? . . . Swiss milk toffee. Well, what a very original suggestion, your Majesty. But I wouldna bother. We aye get plenty toffee fae Mrs. Anderson – the dentist's wife. Fit can ye tak wi' ye then? Tell me now, can ye dae a bilin' o' jam? . . . Oh, ye could . . . Could ye dae rasps? . . . Oh ye couldna . . . Fit's that – ye've nae rasps at Buckingham Palace yonder? God, I thocht ye'd hae a real productive gairden yonder wi' a' that horses gan aboot. Fit could ye dae? Rhubarb? Oh, ye could! Ah weel, jist dae rhubarb. An' dinna forget tae write on yer ticketie – yer sticky label – ER 1975. No, no, yer Majesty, nae Elizabeth Regina. Early Rhubarb.

Now, excuse me for askin', but the wife was wonderin' fit ye would be wearin'? 'Cos she wouldna want tae clash wi' ye. I mean, ye hinna bocht a trooser suit lately, hiv ye – fae C & A? Oh ye hiv! Fit colour is't noo? Oh, that's a' richt then, 'cos hers is reid – wi' yalla flooers. That's the troosers like. The jaicket's white wi' black dots. She files minds me o' a pyoke o' liquorice allsorts.

Well now, that's a wik on Setterday, half past two. I'll meet ye masel' at quarter past two at the crossroads yonder at Drum o' Wartle. Jist by the fillin' station. No, no, yer Majesty, nae the pub. Dinna ging intae the pub or we'll never get ye oot. That's a quarter past two *sharp*. Dinna be late, or ye winna be asked back.

Is yer Mummy in? An appropriate question to put to Prince Edward in 1975.

Jing Bang: Arabic collective noun (cf hillock). As applied to wives, the derivation is too gamey for explanation here, but in the original and purest form the word 'swotta' occurs between 'jing' and 'bang'.

Flora's Letter

Buff, holding a sheet of paper, addresses the audience.

This historical document was discovered on a building site near here. Fortunately, the labourer who found it was a graduate of our university, and he recognised it for what it was – it's a letter, and it's headed – The Far Cuillins, Isle of Skye, 24 October 1746, and it's addressed to The Chairman, Scottish Jacobite Party, Hanover Street, Edinburgh. And it reads:

Dear Sir,
The name Flora MacDonald may not mean anything to you but it does to me because it's my name. I have always been a loyal supporter of Prince Charlie and the Jacobite cause . . . Not anymore. What a man that is! What a man for the drink! When he staggered in tae my hoose efter Culloden, he was stinkin' wi' it. Nae wonder they lost. It'll be a different story now that Ally MacLeod's the manager.

But it's fit happened efter Culloden that I'm complainin' aboot. There was I, ready for my bed, fillin' my warmin' pan, when a knock comes tae the door. I gings tae the door, an' here's this bloke lookin' like David Niven withoot his tache. Well, my cottage is twenty miles fae the nearest village – beggars canna be choosers – so I says 'Come in, come in, it's nice tae see ye. How's yersel, yer lookin' grand.' And he says, 'I'm nae Andy Stewart, I'm Charlie Stuart the Young Pretender.' And I says, 'The Young Pretender? Ye're makin' on.' But no, he wisna. He says, 'I'm fleein'.' I says, 'It's just as weel, ye'll get nothin' tae drink here.' And then he explained, that efter Culloden, he had made a strategic withdrawal – rinnin' for his life doon the West coast. And now he wanted tae get across tae Skye. And he needed a disguise, and he says, 'You must lend me some of your woman's clothing.' I thought, 'Kinky.'

However, I dug oot some o' my aul' claes, and in nae time at a' I had him dressed up like a wifie and lookin' like Stanley Baxter. And then we got intae yon wee boatie – oh, yon was purgatory! Ken this, there's nothin' worse than a person bein' sea-sick, unless it's two persons bein' sea-sick. And as if that wasna bad enough, the water started comin' in ower the boat. So, what did our lad that is born to be king do? He would let the water oot! By removin' the cork fae the bottom o' the boat. As we sank beneath the foamin' brine, I directed towards him a volley, I regret to say, of unpatriotic vituperation. 'Bonnie Prince Charlie', I said, 'Ye're nae bonnie, ye're nae a prince, but what a bloody Charlie!'

Tash Small mouser (see *The Mourners*).

Ally McLeod Dashing Scottish general (Battle honours – Flodden, Culloden, Argentina).

Andy and Charlie Stewart Popular 18th century double-act.

Stanley Baxter Popular 18th century drag act.

'The lad that's born to be king' © Des O'Conner 1987.

Supermarket

Two men, Mr Taylor and Mr Wallace, each pushing a supermarket trolley, enter from opposite sides and meet centre stage.

W.   Hello Mr. Taylor.

T.   Hello Mr. Wallace.

W.   Aye aye.

T.   Aye aye. That's a helluva steer o' folk.

W.   Oh, it's real busy, I will say.

T.   Ye can hardly get moved.

W.   Aye, it's pretty crowded.

T.   Pretty crowded? It's helluva crowded.

W.   Mphph.

T.   Course it's aye the same on a Thursday nicht. Late night shoppin'.

W.   This is true ... This is true.

T.   Well, the last time that I was at Pittodrie, I was at the Beach end at the Celtic match. It wisna half as crowded as this place.

W.   I'll bet it wisna.

T.   I couldna get near the cooked foods.

W.   Is there cooked foods at Pittodrie?

T.   Here! Here!

W.   Oh ... Oh I ken. But did ye try the bakery coonter? The bakery coonter is just seethin'.

T.   I ken, it's bad there an' a'. But it's nae as bad as the cooked foods.

W.   Oh, I dinna ken ...

T. Well, I got my loaf an' my softies …

W. Oh, aye.

T. But I couldna get near the cooked foods, could I?

W. Oh well, Oh well. *(Pause)*

T. I dinna ken far the missus's got till? She went awa' tae the fruit coonter. For twa or three green peppers and an aubergine. An' half a dozen avocado plums.

W. Oh, that's far my wife went til an' a' for a pun' o' cookin' aipples. They must hae just met up. They'll just be stannin' spikkin'.

T. Oh, aye. Spikkin' aboot naethin' at a'. An' gettin' in folks road wi' their trolleys. Oucha! *(He jumps, indicating that someone has bumped into his back with a trolley)* Watch it, watch it!

W. Feel aul' wifey.

T. I see Fairy Liquid's up again.

W. Ye dinna come here for yer Fairy Liquid dae ye?

T. Aye.

W. Oh no! Ye've tae shop aroon' a bit. That's the wye tae make savings. Oh, I comes here for my Penguins an' my Bandits, but I gings tae Coopers for my Fairy Liquid. I gings tae Pick 'n' Save for my fish fingers. Fine Fare for my bacon. Grandfare for my sugar and tea. And oot tae Asda for my cornflakes. And then when I'm oot at Asda, that's when I get my petrol. 'Cos that's where petrol's cheapest.

T. Well it would need tae be. Ye've used a tank o' petrol gettin' oot there.

W. Oh, I never thocht o' that.

T. Ah, well ye see … Tell me, have ye ever gone tae the Co-opie for onything?

W. Oh, aye. Sweeties, lemonade, coca-cola …

T. Coca-cola? I thocht ye said coal! I thocht ye said coal! Well, I've telt ye afore, I would never ging tae the Co-opie for coal!

72

W. Oh I ken, I ken.

T. We used tae get oor coal fae the Co-opie . . . A disaster . . . A disaster! Well, the coal was aye weet.

W. Oh it's disappointin' that though! Mind you, of course, ye should have got the Shilbottle.

T. We did get the Shilbottle. An' the Shilbottle was weeter than ony o' them! I'll tell ye foo weet it was. We had tae put half the load in the spin drier!

W. Oh, gee, that is weet that, though!

T. Well it didna dae wir sheets ony good.

W. No, I'll bet it didna!

T. Here, div you ever get the feelin' that we've been here afore?

W. Well, it's possible . . . I come here maist Thursday nichts. 'Cos it's late night shoppin' ye see. If ye come on a Wednesday, the shop's closed. Usually. I mind once comin' on a Wednesday and it was open, but that was because it was Hogmanay. That's the reason.

T. Aha, but was it? I mean, was it open on the Wednesday because it was Hogmanay or because the next day, the Thursday, was New Year's day, a holiday? And it was gan tae be closed?

W. Eh?

T. Well, pit it this wye, If the Thursday hidna been New Year's day an' a holiday, would this place still have been open on the Wednesday, just because it was Hogmanay?

W. I dinna ken onything aboot that kind o' thing.

T. I tell ye one good thing aboot late night shoppin'. Ye see a lot o' folk ye ken. I've just seen Charlie and Betty Ironside.

W. 'Course, Hogmanay sometimes lands on a Sunday. *(Mr Taylor gapes at him, incredulous)*

T. I said I've just seen Charlie and Betty Ironside ... ower aside the cat foods.

W. Oh, have they got a cat noo? ... I aye thought they had a dog.

T. They have got a dog! But they feed it on cat food. It's cheaper.

W. Ah. ... Are ye allowed tae dae that?

T. Allowed tae dae fit?

W. Feed cat food tae a dog?

T. Well it's a' richt as lang as the dog disna tell onybody. Like phonin' up the Cruelty.

W. They shouldna come here for their cat food onywye. It's much cheaper at Pets' Puntry. I aye go tae Pets' Puntry on my wye oot tae Asda.

T. But have you got ony pets?

W. No, I just likes the bargains.

T. Tell me, is Pets' Puntry ony good for budgie seed?

W. Oh aye, but did you nae loss your budgie?

T. Och aye, we lost oor budgie the nicht o' the big blitz.

W. I thocht that now!

T. But we got a new een.

W. Oh?

T.   We got a new een twa wiks ago. Fae a place oot at Torphins.

W.   Was it delivered?

T.   No it wisna delivered, it was hatched. Ye see ye dinna deliver budgies. A budgie's a bird.

W.   That's an awfy lot o' toilet rolls ye've got there Mr. Taylor! Is a'body fine?

T.   Oh aye, we're a' richt. But the budgie's a bit seedy.

W.   Oh ... Oh ... I'm sorry tae hear that!

T.   Look I'd better awa' an' find Mrs. Taylor before she buys up the hale shop.

W.   Aye, weel, but ye'll hae tae come roond some nicht. You an' Mrs. Taylor.

T.   Weel, that would be fine. But I'll phone you, O.K.?

W.   Aye, Uhuh. We'll get a' yer news.

T.   Aye, there must be a lot tae catch up on. *(Mr Taylor wanders away)*

W.   We'll just sit roond the fire an' hae a few laughs ... Mind you, he hasna much o' a sense o' humour, Mr. Taylor.

Jimmy Carter   (AG)

P.A. Voice: Good Evening. And it's over live now to Aberdeen where they've been having local elections. And in one ward, the votes of twelve American residents were enough to elect their own candidate who is now running for Lord Provost of the city.

Jimmy Carter: Ma name is Jimmy Carter and I'm running for provost. Friends, I believe, in this great city of . . . Aberdeen. I've spent the last four months putting America in order . . . Aberdeen will take a little longer. Friends and fellow carters, the American Declaration of Independence was written two hundred years ago, at a time when George Washington had just begun what was to become the greatest and the best ice-cream soda fountain at the beach. Next to the Inversnecky.

In that same year Aberdeen's own constitution was written, known as the corporation by-laws, and I quote one of its fundamental principles, sub section 2/1. 'Every citizen, whatever his race, creed or colour, shall own a bucket.' Friends, I believe in the buckets of this city, because the buckets of this city are a symbol, a symbol of a city that casts out its garbage and holds unto itself only that which is clean and pure.

Friends, last night, as I was a-walking the granite moonlit streets, I heard the clock of the West Church of St. Nicholas a-chiming out twelve times. And I fell to thinking – must be about nine o'clock. And back home in Plains, Georgia, my mother, Miss Lilian Carter, she was putting out her bucket. Stupid old fool, it's the middle of the afternoon there.

Friends, my main concern is for the deprived and underprivileged citizens of my old ward, Rubislaw. And so I pledge myself that every house in Rubislaw Den will have an inside john. I dedicate myself to getting the roads sanded within three days of the snow falling. I commit myself to widening Union Street to a dual carriageway and widening George's Street to a single carriageway. As leader of Aberdeen District, I will pursue a policy of detente with the other great super power, Grampian Region, and their convenor, Chairman Mutch. For District and Region must live together in peace and harmony, they must love each other, they must respect each other, they must trust each other, no matter how crooked the Region may be.

Turning now to the main issue of this campaign, I believe the chairs in the new Town House must be appropriate to the dignity of the councillors, and so to buy these chairs, I will reopen Cocky Hunters. I will protect the interests of minority groups such as the Norco House Preservation Society, the Claben Madrigal Society, the Friends of Mounthooly Roundabout, the Teetotalers

Section of the British Legion. Friends, I believe in the people of this city, the folk of this city. Because the folk of this city are good folk. Honest folk, caring folk, loving folk and sharing folk, folk from Constitution St. and folk from Rubislaw Den, I love you all.

Thank you

Bucket Georgian trash-can.

John Georgian watery.

Cocky Hunter Conceited Aberdeen junk-merchant.

The Adjudicator

Adjudicator: I suppose it can only be regarded as one of the more unfortunate incidents in this year's Amateur Drama Festival that the record of Greig's *Peter Gynt Suite* was broken during the dress rehearsal, because quite honestly, the ethos of Ibsen's play wasn't wholly captured by the only other record available, *Jimmy Shand's Hogmanay Party*.

Next, the Gardenstown Thespians' production of *Oh Calcutta!*. Or to give it their own sub-title, the Dirtiest Show in Banff and Buchan. Come on now Gardenstown, you can be dirtier than that.

So then to the final entry, the Crathie Parish Church Amateur Dramatic Club's offering of *Othello*. Or as it was pronounced during the entire course of the evening, Oh Hello. Whether this was a suitable choice of play for an all female society is somewhat open to question. For instance, I did have a wee qualm, just a whisper of a doubt, about the wisdom of casting Mrs. MacIntosh, the minister's wife, as Othello, simply on the strength of her admittedly very striking resemblance to General Idi Amin, in one of his more murderous postures. As for Desdemona, well I hesitate to suggest that Granny Thomson from the sweetie shop was miscast in this part. I agree she is a very young seventy-five, but you know, I did find it just a little bit difficult to accept that she and Mrs MacIntosh were actually husband and wife. Not enough passion in the embraces, not enough conviction in the clinches somehow. Not Granny's fault; she did get her teeth into the part. It's just a pity she hadn't kept them in her mouth where they belong.

I must pass over the rest of the cast for the sake of brevity and charity, and move on to the producer who deserves a meed of praise for his unusual interpretation. It's the first time I've seen *Othello* played for laughs. An unusual touch too, was the inclusion of the specially composed musical numbers. For instance, the jolly singing of the bothy ballad in Desdemona's death scene soon had everybody's feet tapping, including the deceased Desdemona, and cheered us all up no end.

A word about the splendid diction of Miss Eileen Webster, the prompter. Eileen could be heard right at the back of the hall, and she deserves a very special pat on the back – fairly low down. A word also about the stage manager, who was undoubtedly the best I've ever seen – and I saw him at least six times. These are minor quibbles however, the churlish strictures of a cynical old pro.

By and large this is a production which will not be readily forgotten. Which is more than can be said for most of Othello's lines and practically all of Desdemona's. So then, to the Crathie Parish Church, goes the Walter Carr Rose

Bowl. And to Granny Thomson for her magnificent portrayal of Desdemona, the individual award, which this year takes the form of a night out with Howard M. Lockhart.

General Idi Amin Ugandan actor, early exponent of theatre in the round.

WE'RE NO' AWA' TAE BIDE AWA'

VARIATION 2 ~ BEETHOVEN

82

VARIATION 3 ~ MOZART

VARIATION 4 ~ HANDEL

The Prize-Giving

A pompous man wearing a red gown and a chain denoting some municipal office is addressing an audience.

My Lord Provost, Chairman of Governors, Reverend Sir, Headmaster and masters, parents, boys of the school, janitor . . . Now it's a great pleasure and privilege for you tae hae me here the day at this yer annual prize-giving, to present the prize-winners with their prizes. But before doing so, perhaps I may be allowed to vouchsafe a few words of advice mined from the harvest fields of my own experience.

Now, we've all went tae the school. But some of us has went longer than others. But I regret to say I was not one. I left school early, usually aboot three o'clock, being excused arithmetic on religious grounds. And I went straight from school to the university. But my university, boys, was the university of life, necessity my teacher, my classroom the gutter, from which it has been a lang road, not without squalls and laden with hurdles, which I have had to plough, before breasting the tape of success, achieving my goal an' bein' asked along here this efterneen.

An' fit a rare efterneen it's been. The choir's rendering of *The Skye Boat Song* gets better every year, though I did think the retiral of Miss Nicholson, the Botany mistress, had left the choir somewhat short of baritones. A great character, Miss Nicholson. 'Knickers' as the boys called her. Inaccurately, the headmaster tells me.

The headmaster's own report on the year's activities was a topper and I was delighted tae hear the silence with which it was received with. Very gratifying to hear that the school is in such good heart. Better heart, if ye ask me, than the school I've sent my twa loons til, Fettes College, Edinburgh. Do you know, ladies and gentlemen, that there are boys leaving Fettes College today who don't even have a trade! *(He produces a newspaper cutting).* This is the *Edinburgh Evening News* for 17 July. City and Guilds examination results, in Plumbing, Joinery and Butchery. Not a single Fettes boy in the pass list. And only one Loretto!

But now, tae the main business o' the efterneen, the presentation o' the prizes tae the clever eens. But to the many boys here today who will not receive a prize I would say this. I never won a prize in my life, but ootside the door of this hall, there stands a gleaming Rolls Royce. And do you know who that belongs to boys? It belongs to me. And it carries me between the biggest hoose in this city and the biggest mealie puddin' factory in this city, from which a fleet of vans all bearing my name, go forth daily, bringing mealie puddings to your dinner tables and champagne and caviare to mine. So you see, I have got all that is best out of this life, not by being a brilliant scholar, but by observing a few homespun rules: never trust nobody, never share nothing... or you'll never get nowhere. This boys, is the things to remember when you have forgot every word of Rembrandt you was ever learned.

Now to the presentation. The headmaster will hand over the books as I shout out the names. Now the first prize, for primary 1A, is David Copperfield. Come away up David.

Fettes College Grim Victorian penitentiary near Pilton.

Loretto Even grimmer Victorian penitentiary.

Mealie pudding White jimmic, or in Aberdeen, a tennis shoe (see *Wedding Guests*).

The Return of Bruce and the Spider

The year is 1314, and Mr. Robertson is a spider. But it is now two days after Bannock-burn. (The Spider is discovered, reading the Press and Journal)

S. Land o' the shining river, land o' my high endeavour, land o' my he'rt forever – Scotland. Oh, I'm chuffed. Oh I feel richt prood. After a' these years o' failure. Try, try, try again. I'm the first spider ever tae win Fix the Ba'. Fit else is in the paper the day, eh? 'Great Scottish victory,' it says, 'Bannockburn Special. by Alastair MacDonald.' Oh this'll be good this, eh? Oh me, there's a pictur o' a mannie wi' a spear sticking oot o' him and bleed a' wye. Oh that's horrible that! Oh, here's another een wi' his heid aff! Oh, it'll be Fix the Heid next wik. Fit's Alastair saying aboot it though, eh? 'At Bannockburn Stadium today, an under-strength Scottish army, went to town against their more fancied opponents.' He disna pull any punches, Alastair, does he? 'After the debaucle England team manager, King Edward II., told reporters 'I am dissatisfied with my squad's performance, and there will have to be changes in the line-up before the Hundred Years War. The English team boss criticised the Scottish army for poor sportsmanship, including time-wasting and bad language. Fit a bluidy cheek! At this, Scottish supremo, Robert the Bruce, lashed oot.' Dinna blame him! 'And in so doing, took aff the leg o' the English trainer.' Oh, Gad sakes, that's horrible that!

(Enter Bruce)

B. Easy, easy, easy, easy. We are the people.

S. Oh me! It's Brucie, didn't he do well! Here, Robert, I've just been readin' aboot you. That wis two good points you got the day.

B. Aye, my friend, it was a famous victory. Now the Bannockburn runs red swollen wi' English bleed.

S. Oh, dinna you start for ony sake!

B. Three-one was the score, and England's goal was a penalty.

S. Oh, but I telt ye ye were tae win, didn't I Robert?

B. Yes ye did, an' for a' ye've done for Scotland I'm here tae invite ye tae a booze-up at the committee rooms a wik on Tuesday. Seven for seven-thirty, bar open at 3.00pm.

S. Oh, but Tuesday's nae a good night for me. Tuesday I gings tae an evening class. Advanced spinning and weaving.

B. Well, what nicht would suit ye?

S. I will consult my diary. *The Arachnids' Almanac.* Well now, on Monday, I've got my masons.

B. Is there a lodge for spiders?

S. Oh well, we just ging in wi' the slaters.

B. Well, what aboot Wednesday?

S. Wednesday? Oh, I've got a beetle drive. Thursday's late night shoppin, an' Friday, now fit have I got on a Friday? Oh, I've got my Dancing.

B. Your Dancing?

S. Ye askin'? No, no, I've got a special dancing class for spiders.

B. What's special aboot a dancing class for spiders?

S. Ye only need one couple for an eightsome reel.

B. So you enjoy Scottish dancing?

S. Oh aye, and I enjoys a tarantula.

B. Na, na, ye mean a tarantella. You wouldna enjoy a tarantula, that's an exotic black widow from South America.

S. That's richt, I enjoys a tarantula.

B. Well, it looks as if you're a' booked up next wik. And the wik efter that I'm awa mysel. I'm due ower the border, intae England, for a bittie pilage and rape.

S. Oh, very nice! Oh, of course, it's the Trades Fortnicht.

B. Well now, seein' ye canna manage the booze-up, a grateful nation would wish you to have some tangible reward. What would ye like oot o' this clubbie book? I mean would you like something for your larder? What aboot some flies?

S. Oh, I've plenty flies, I've got household flies, I've got horse-flies, I've got dragon-flies.

B. Have ye got green-flies?

S. It just depends fit suit I'm wearing.

B. Now my freend, I must awa'. I've a lang wye tae go, through the mist and the rain.

S. Oh, is it raining? Oh me, somebody's squashed anither o' my chums!

B. And now, as the sun sets on this great victory, a new dawn breaks for Scotland.

S. Oh, you're for devolution, are ye?

B. I'm nae sure.

S. Oh! Robert the Bruce is a don't know. Oh well, ye'd better nae tell Margo Macdonald aboot it. Or ye'll get yer heid in yer hands.

B. But what I want ye tae tell me now is – are you for devolution?

S. Oh, aye, I am pro-devolutionist.

B. Well, but are ye sure Scotland's ready for it?

S. Oh aye, have ye nae heard what they've discovered off Peterheid?

B. What? In the sea?

S. Oh no, there's nothing in the sea. There's just a pucklie fish in the sea. No, no, at the other side, roon aboot Lonmay and Mintlaw.

B. What have they discovered?

S. Tatties.

B. Tatties!

S. Aye, tatties. Vast deposits o' tatties.

B. But fa's tatties are they?

S. They're Scotland's tatties

B. Scotland's tatties!

S. Aye.

B. Ye mean we can tell the Arabs fit tae dee wi' their tatties?

S. We'll have mair tatties than the Arabs and the Jews pit thegither.

B. Aye my freend, an' in years tae come folk'll sing aboot Scotland's tatties.

S. That's right!

B. Aye, I can hear it now.

S. *The Tatties o' Scotland* sung by the Rubislaw Corries

(Guitars have miraculously materialised, and they sing to the tune of Flower of Scotland*)*

> The tatties of Scotland
> How proudly grow the tattie shaws
> They're Scotland's tatties
> Untouched by English laws
> They're very tasty
> Wi' beef or pork
> Kerr's Pink, King Edward
> And Duke of York.
>
> Roast, mashed or sauté
> The Scottish tottie
> Taks the cake
> But what of the stovies
> Yer mammy used tae make?
> Or else we bile them,
> But tak it fae me
> If you're no careful
> They're through the bree.

Alastair MacDonald *Press and Journal* war correspondent, 1314.

The Councillor

D.C. Thank you very much ladies and gentlemen for coming along to this inaugurational meeting in my campaign for re-election to the District Cooncil. Now this is what democracy is all about, me the Cooncillor, coming face to face with you, the punters. Now, I'm nae gonna try the nicht tae dazzle ye wi' the brilliance o' my rhetoric. I'm nae here tae mak a speech or bum ma load or nothing. The object of the exercise this evening, is for to have a meaningful dialogue between civilised human beings – sit doon an' shut yer face! Sit doon, sit doon, you'll get yer shottie, you'll get yer shottie. If you've got a question, raise your hand, state your name and address, and in the case of that young lady there, your phone number an' a'. It's a' richt darlin', I'm just jokin'.

Could we have the first question please?

Con. 1. Douglas Adams of 36, Calsayseat Road.

D.C. Yes Mr. Adams?

Con. 1. What are the Councillor's views on the criteria used by the government to determine the level of rate support grant to local authorities?

D.C. Did you say 36, Calsayseat Road?

Con. 1. Yes.

D.C. You'll ken Bill Peters. He bides at thirty-eight. Ye ken Bill? Give him my warmest regards. Thank you very much for your question Mr. Adams.

Con. 1. But what about the rate support grant, councillor? Have you any views on that?

D.C. Yes, I do have views on that. Next question please?

Con. 2. Councillor, we hear a lot aboot corruption and graft in local government. Now I ken for a fact that your sixteen-year-auld nephew has got a pensioner's concessionary ticket on the buses.

D.C. So, so?

Con. 2. So do you think that's fair?

D.C. Nothing unfair aboot it, his wee brother's got the same. But since you have raised the question of morality in public life. I'm well aware that there is a lot of allegations being pit aboot, by a number of alligators, that my wife was expectin' when we got mairried. It's nae true. The bairn was three-year-auld. Yes, aye, the gentleman there wi' the baldie heid an' the reid nose.

Con. 3. Councillor, a question about housing.

D.C. Housing? Yes!

Con. 3. Well now, my Granny is aged eighty-three. Now how can my Granny get a low door?

D.C. How can your Granny get a low door? She's nae a dwarf, is she? Something better than that, something better than that, come on! Yes, sir?

Con. 4. Councillor, your election circular describes you as Alexander Swick P.H.D.

D.C. P.H.D., Yes?

Con. 4. Now, does P.H.D. stand for Doctor of Philosophy?

D.C. No. Peterheid. Peterheid, the place of my birth. Then when I wis three-year-auld my parents got a shift. Fan they were cuttin' doon on staff at the prison.

Con. 4. Your father was a warder?

D.C. No, my mither.

Con. 4. Would you therefore agree Councillor that you are not a true Aberdonian?

D.C. Do I hear the voice of prejudice and racism, raised here in Kitty-brewster School? I would have you know, squire, that in this great country of ours, a man is not to be judged by his place of birth, his race, creed or colour. Now, there's a Chinkie mannie at the back got a question. Come away, Who-Flung-Dung, come on. Would I be right in thinking you are a member of the catering profession? . . . You're a Professor of Nuclear Physics! I see, I see. Well now, professor, Fit is it ye're nae sure aboot?

Con. 5. Old Chinese proverb say 'Mony a mickle mak a muckle.'

93

D.C. That's nae a Chinese proverb! That's oor proverb that! Bloomin' chick. Bloomin' Chinese, comin' ower here, pinchin' wir proverbs! Takin' ower wir chip shops, jeopardisin' the livelihood o' wir ain native born Italians. Bloomin' disgrace. Next question, next question.

Con. 6. Councillor, it's been proposed that a section of Aberdeen beach should be reserved for nudists.

D.C. Far are ye? Far are ye?

Con. 6. Over here councillor, over here.

D.C. Oh yes, the gentleman in the dirty raincoat. Yes? Your question again please?

Con. 6. What do you think about having private sections of the beach for nudists?

D.C. Nudists? Well, there's a few wyes o' lookin' at this. But, there is a fair measure of agreement between the two major parties, Councillor Collie and myself. We think the pair o' us should be sent on an all expenses paid study tour of the nudist beaches of the Mediterranean. Now this would not be a skive at the ratepayers expense. We would both have very specific briefs. Yes, one last question?

Con. 7. Eh, councillor, I'm anxious to know what your political affiliations are? Now, what is the significance of that red rosette you are wearing?

D.C. This here? I hinna been able to get it oot o' my jaiket since the League Cup Final.

Councillor Swick Swick: v.t. (N.E.) to cheat, deceive.

Low door An expression used in Aberdeen to denote a house with its external access at ground level. The door itself can be any height you like as long as it's low.

94

The Beechgrove Garden

We hear The Beechgrove Garden *signature tune as the camera zooms in on George Barron and Jim McColl who are standing in a corner of the garden sheltering under a golf umbrella.*

J. Hello, well welcome once again to the Beechgrove Garden, where, as you can see, it's a lovely day.

G. Aye, there's just been the one shower the day. It started at breakfast time, and it's still going on.

J. Now we'd like today to deal with what many people regard as the most important part of any day in the garden, the fly-cup, yer cuppie o' tea, the tea-break, call it what you will. Now George, you're a man who's had a pucklie fly-cups in his day.

G. Aye hiv ah, aye hiv ah. But it disna matter foo mony fly-cups ye've had in your time, as a gairdner, every one is a new experience.

J. Now, we realise that many of our viewers will never have had the nerve to have a go at their own fly-cup, so George, what would your advice be to the beginner?

G. Well, as in all aspects of gardening, preparation is the key.

J. Preparation. Now is preparation for the fly-cup a dirty job?

G. No, it's a clean job really because it's just washing your hands. Because workin' aboot in the gairden yonder yer hands do get real fool working wi' a' yon . . .

J. Yes, I think the viewers can see all that – all that's happening. Now, when we wash our hands, in preparation for the fly-cup, what would you recommend us to use?

G. Well of course, there's a lot of very good proprietary substances on the market nowadays, but I still prefers soap.

J. Soap?

G. Soap.

J. Now is that easily obtainable?

G. Oh ye can pick it up onywye. In ony hotel bathroom or ye can even buy it.

J. Good, no problems there, so hands are now clean. What next?

G. Well this is where you get your equipment thegither. Ye've got yer kettle, yer mug and yer tea pot.

J. Now, not a saucer?

G. No! no, no, nae a saucer. As you ken Jim, I used to tak my tea oot o' a saucer – the same as you – but we were baith telt nae tae dae it on the television.

J. Well I think we can get the brolley down now, the rain seems to have eased off. Well if I could pick up the story from there. The next thing is to fill the kettle with water, heat it to a temperature of 212° Farenheit, that's 100° Celsius, pour the water from the kettle into the tea-pot into which you have already put two tea-bags.

G. Aye, aye. Now of course, there is a lot of very good pre-packed bags on the market nowadays. I mean, baith Typhoo and Fisons do a very good bag.

J. Well, if you've followed the procedures we've described so far, you should now have a pot of tea.

G. Aye now, of course, this is a different kind o' pot from the ither pots that you use in the gairden.

J. A very good point George. Yes, this is not a common or garden pot.

G. No, it's nae a garden pot at a'. Because a garden pot has got a hole in the bottom. And if you try to use a pot with a hole in the bottom, oh, it wid be nae use for haudin' yer tea at a'. No, no.

J. Well thank you very much George, for that very useful tip. Well worth bearing in mind. Now, the tea is ready to drink, although some gardeners do like to add some bovine lactial fluid and some crystallised sucrose granuals. Do *you* do that George?

G. No, I prefers milk and sugar masel'.

J. Well, we can move on now to the second essential element of any fly-cup and this is, of course, the piece.

G. The piece.

J. The piece.

G. The piece.

J. The piece. Now, George here has left his piece on the top of the cold frame in another part of the garden.

G. Aye hiv I. I have left my piece in another part of the garden, an' I think we micht just take a timmer ower and see how my piece is getting on, on top of the cold frame . . . in another . . . part of the . . . garden.

J. Very good. *(They walk through the garden; Jim points towards a flower bed)* Well George, the roses are doing well?

G. Aye, oh aye.

J. Where did you get your roses from? Was it Andersons?

G. No, Anderson Drive.

J. Now, that's a fine show there, the pink and the blue. What's that?

G. Oh now, that's the sweet peas, that.

J. And behind them, the green and the yellow? What's that?

G. Oh that's the top o' a Midstocket bus.

J. Well here we are now at the cold frame, and here we have George's piece.

G. Now, this is a very good example of a piece, this. It's a slice of loaf, and it's spread evenly wi' butter, and jeely. Now that's the jeely on top o' the butter.

J. The jeely on top o' the butter.

G. The jeely on top o' the butter.

J. And over here you have another slice spread exactly the same.

G. Aye hiv I, aye hiv I. It's just exactly the same that, Jim.

J. And what's that for?

97

G. That is . . . in case I'm hungry.

J. And is that slice from the same loaf as this one?

G. Aye is't, Aye is't. In this case it is, but it disna need tae be the same loaf. It's in your ain option. And it gives you a choice, because you have either got two jeely pieces or one *(slaps the two together)* sandwich. *(Jim removes a flying piece of jam from his eye)*

J. Well thank you very much, George. And as time catches up with us once again, the sun comes breaking through, always a welcome sight for any gardener.

G. Aye, I've said it before Jim, and I'll say it again. Give me sunshine.

(To the music of Give me Sunshine *they turn and dance off* à la Morecambe *and Wise).*

Fit D'Ye Ca' 'Im

Mr Sharp and Mr Bell meet in Union Street.

S.   I wis spikkin tae . . . Fit d'ye ca' 'im? . . . Last eh . . .

B.   Fa?

S.   Ken . . . the boy . . . thingummy.

B.   Oh, him.

S.   Aye.

B.   Gee whiz, I hinna seen him for . . . oh . . .

S.   Weel neither had I.

B.   Foo's he daein'?

S.   Oh, nae great.

B.   Nae great?

S.   Nae great. ken he used tae be wi' . . . eh . . .

B.   Aye, across the road fae . . .

S.   Weel he fair blotted his copy book there . . .

B.   Is that so?

S.   Oh, he made a richt thingummy o' it.

B.   Did he?

S.   Oh, aye.

B.   But he couldna hae been there very lang I would say he was only there aboot . . . oh . . .

S.   Oh, nae as lang as that

B.   And he's really got the . . .

S. Ho ho, ho ho and how . . . This is fit he was tellin' me. Books. Wik's wages. Good night, sweetheart.

B. Ho, ho, ho, ho, ho. But ye shouldna laugh, though.

S. Ye shouldna laugh.

B. I'll tell ye fa I'm sorry for . . . I'm sorry for his . . . eh . . .

S. For his eh . . . ?

B. His eh . . . ?

S. Oh, but she had left him by that time!

B. Had she?

S. Aye. 'Cos he'd started messin' aboot. Wi, eh . . . wi' eh . . .

B. Oh, nae wi' her! . . . I mean, she used tae shack up wi' yon . . . *(adopts ape-like posture)*

S. That's richt, weel she was still shackin' up wi yon . . . *(adopts similar posture)*

B. He wisna feart, was he?

S. He was not . . .

B. So fit did he dee efter he . . . ?

S. This is fit he was tellin' me. Then he tried tae start up his ain . . . eh . . .

B. Did he?

S. Aye.

B. Far aboot?

S. Well, ken? Along the road fae . . . Doon fae . . . Roon the corner fae . . . eh . . . there's a little . . .

B. Oh, it's him that wis in there, wis it?

S. Aye.

B. Well, but he couldna hae been there very lang either, 'cos it was ta'en ower by the . . .

S. That's richt, . . . that's richt . . .

B. By the thingummy . . . And then it was fit ye ca' 'im that had it . . .

S. Aye, aye.

B. And we ken fit happened tae him . . .

S. Aye, 'cos we was baith at his . . . eh . . .

B. That's richt, that's richt, . . . the wik afore the . . .

S. Oh no, it was the wik efter the . . . eh . . .

B. The wik efter! You're quite right, the wik efter! Fit wye did I think it was the wik afore?

S. The wik afore was the wik that . . . eh . .

B. Ah well, never mind aboot that . . . fit happened til him efter he had tae . . .

S. This is fit he was tellin' me . . . then he got in wi' . . . eh . . .

B. In wi' fa'?

S. In wi' . . . eh . . .

B. Oh, aye, I did hear that . . .

S. And then of course they went . . .

B. They went an' a'?

S. They went an' a'!

B. Oh gee . . .

S. Aye, an' then of course he had tae sell up his . . .

B. Of course.

S. Alang in . . .

101

B. Aye, aye.

S. And he couldna keep up the . . .

B. Of course he couldna.

S. So they took awa' his . . .

B. They didna take that awa'?

S. Aye.

B. I mean, that was his hale . . .

S. I ken.

B. Ken? So, fit's he daein' noo?

S. This is fit he was tellin' me. He had tae move in wi' his . . .

B. Oh . . . Nae wi' her .

S. Aye!

B. I mean, she's got five . . .

S. Six! The last een was twins.

B. But she ta'en him in!

S. But she ta'en him in! She ta'en him in! . . . Weel ye ken fit they say? Fit ye ca' it's thicker than thingummy.

B. You never said a truer word.

S. Weel, weel, but I'll need tae awa' . . . Cheerio Stan.

B. Cheerio Stan? I'm nae Stan! I thocht it was Stan we wis spikkin' aboot!

The Sleeper

A railway sleeper, occupied by two passengers. Mr Sim occupies the lower berth, Mr Brown is fast asleep on the upper berth.

S.   I can never get tae sleep in a sleeper ... Can you?

B.   Zzzzzzzzzz.

S.   I said I can never get tae sleep in a sleeper ... Can you? ...

B.   Eh! Fit's 'at?

S.   I said I can never get tae sleep in a sleeper ... Can you?

B.   Oh, I'm sorry! I didna hear ye, I was fast asleep.

S.   Oh, you're lucky, you must be used til't. You must ging tae London a lot, div ye?

B.   Oh aye, I'm up and doon a' the time. Goodnight.

S.   I ken fit wye we canna get tae sleep!

B.   Fit dae ye mean, *WE* canna get tae sleep? I was sleepin' fine when you shouted up!

S.   Oh, I'm sorry. I'm sorry, but I'm just plottin' doon here! Fit a heat there is in this place ... I'm just puggled.

B.   Well, ye see that nozzle thing? That nozzle. That's the air conditionin'.

S.   This thing here wi' the hot air comin' oot?

B.   Is there hot air comin' oot?

S.   Aye.

B.   Well, turn it tae caul'!

S.   It is at caul'! ... Ye're nae really sleepin', are ye?

B.   Aye, I'm sleepin'.

S.   Ye are not sleepin'.

103

B. I am so sleepin'. Can ye nae hear I'm sleepin'? Zzzzzzzz.

S. D'ye ken fit I'm gan doon tae London for?

B. No.

S. I'm gan doon for the El Alamein Reunion.

B. Wir you at Alamein, then?

S. No, but my brither wis. He bides in Battersea.

B. He'd a lang wye tae ging tae Alamein, then.

S. I saw in a documentary on the TV that Alamein wis the turnin' point o' the war.

B. 'At's richt. Efter Alamein Monty had control of the desert.

S. 'At's richt. Monty had control o' the desert. Fit good did that dae, though? Haein' control o' a' that sand?

B. Well, if Monty hidna had control o' a' that sand, the Germans wid hiv hid control o' it. And then far wid you be now?

S. Well, I widna be in this bloomin' sleeper. Ye wouldna hae naething tae eat, would ye?

B. No.

S. I made a big mistake. I thocht there was a diner on this train! So I never had my tea nor naethin'!

B. Oh, I'm sorry, I had a big tea afore I came doon tae the station.

S. Did ye?

B. I had yalla fish and a poached egg.

S. Oh, dinna.

B. Then twa softies and syrup and a couple o' Club biscuits.

S. Oh, that sounds affa fine! Just ane o' yer softies would hae deen me.

B. And then the wife drove me doon tae the station in the car. That was her that was seein' me aff. Did your wife see you aff?

S. Oh no, she would never come tae the station.

B. Oh, does she nae like farewells?

S. No, she widna miss Coronation St. Are ye sure ye hinna even a sweetie or naethin'? I'm just starving!

B. No, I'm sorry, but look, ye'll be a' richt, they'll waken ye up wi' a cup o' tea in the mornin'.

S. Will they?

B. Aye, a cup o' tea and a puckly custard creams aboot quarter tae four.

S. I dinna think I'll last oot till a quarter tae four. Can I nae get a cup o' tea fae the boy, the attendant, before he gings tae sleep?

B. Fit dae ye mean, 'gings tae sleep?' He was fast asleep when we got on the train. Onywye, the sleepin' car attendants is haein' a go slow this wik. It's their shottie. That boy we've got, he's gan' that slow, if he started makin' yer tea now, ye widna get it till Peterborough.

S. Oh, me, I'm richt thirsty. Is there nae a drink o' water onywye? Far's the washhand basin for ony sake?

B. Ye see that shelf ye pit yer kitbag on? If ye open up the lid o' that, ye'll find the washhand basin and certain other facilities. But ye've tae watch it, that's nae drinkin' water! Look, it says 'Nae Drinkin' Water'.

S. 'Nae Drinkin' Water' ... Ye're nae allowed tae drink the water?

B. Nae allowed tae drink the water.

S. Oh me!

B. But ye can clean yer teeth in it.

S. Clean my teeth! Fit would I want tae clean my teeth for? I hinna had naethin' tae eat!

B. I thocht a Desert Rat like you could survive onywye.

S. I dinna think a camel would survive on this train. Has there ever been a case o' a deid camel bein' ta'en aff the train at King's Cross?

105

B. Look, if ye really want a drink, open that little cupboard there, and you'll find an ice-cold bottle of luke-warm Schweppes. It's safe enough.

S. Oh, it's safe enough, there's nothin' in't!

B. It's nae your lucky night is't?

S. You wouldna hae onything tae read, would ye?

B. No.

S. I wonder if there's onything worth readin' in my wallet? . . . Oh, here's my driving licence. I hinna read that for a while. Oh me, it's expired!

B. Just as weel ye're on a train then.

S. Oh me, what a place this is! Far are we onywye? We surely hinna far tae ging have we?

B. Wait a minute, I'll hae a look, Oh, were gettin' on. We're gettin' on. There's a stretch o' water. We must be helluva near Montrose.

S. MONTROSE!

B. Och, come on, cheer up man, cheer up. I aye enjoy it in a sleeper. I think it's very clever the wye these sleepers are designed wi' a' the shelves and cupboards. Very clever, I think.

S. Clever, it's nae sae clever. I'll tell you, boy, ten minutes ago I thocht that was a cupboard up there and I threw my galluses oot the windae!

B. Ah well, I mean, that's just bad luck, is't?

S. Bad luck? It's worse than bad luck, they were fastened on tae ma briks.

Plotin' Conspirin', i.e. posh word for 'sweatin''

Puggled Past participle of 'plottin''.

Softie A species of Aberdeen bun, slightly sweeter than, but to most refined palates, inferior to its cousin the stewie bap.

Camel The ship of the desert, not surprisingly less suited to rail than sea travel.

Evening Express Popular brand of fire-lighter in Aberdeen.

'IT GETS YE OOT O' THE HOOSE'

♩ = 132 *(with a mixture of relief and disillusionment)*

Hame fae yer work, sit doon tae yer tea,

Read the pap-er, an' watch T. V.; Drink yer co—coa, pit oot the cat —

There must be mair to life than that. On—y int'—rest ye care tae choose, As

lang's it gets ye oot o' the hoose. For ex——am-ple we go jog-ging, it's a

♩ = 100 *jauntily*

healthy thing to do. The experts say if ye jog each day, Ye'll live till ye're ninety-two. But I gasp for breath & I

108

feel like death & I turn a shade of puce_____. Jog-gin's real-ly mur-der, but it

Fine

gets ye oot o' the hoose. There's jog-gers ly-in' ill in moist wards in For'-ster—

hill, an' we must ad-mit it's kil—lin; But it gets ye oot o' the hoose.

It Gets Ye Oot o' the Hoose

Hame fae yer work, sit doon tae yer tea,
Read the paper, an' watch T.V.;
Drink yer cocoa, pit oot the cat –
There must be mair tae life than that.

The secret is tae hae a pursuit –
A pastime, a hobby that takes ye oot,
Ony interest ye care tae choose,
As lang's it gets ye oot o' the hoose.

For example we go jogging – it's a healthy thing to do.
The experts say if ye jog each day
Ye'll live till ye're ninety-two.
But I gasp for breath,
I feel like death,
I turn a shade of puce.
Jogging's really murder, but
It gets ye oot o' the hoose.

There's joggers lyin' ill in
Maist wards in For'sterhill, an'
We must admit it's killin',
But it gets ye oot o' the hoose.

I ging tae Old Time Dancin' – I cheerfully embark
On an old-time waltz in a hall in Cults
Overlookin' the Allan Park.
But I lose the beat, I've got twa left feet,
And though I look quite spruce,
I canna dance for toffee, but
It gets me oot o' the hoose.

He's nae a Fred Astaire,
His dancin's less than fair,
An' it maks my ankles sair,
But it gets ye oot o' the hoose.

In the Territorial Army we serve our gracious Queen,
With rifle and Bren we're a body of men
Whose like you've never seen,
But the weapons in the main that we use when we train
Went oot wi' Robert the Bruce;
We're only playin' at sodgers, but
It gets ye oot o' the hoose.

110

They march him up tae Tain, an'
They gie him battle trainin',
An the hale wik-end it's rainin',
But it gets ye oot o' the hoose.

I'm een o' the lads that plays in the Mannofield Pipe Band,
And the swing o' the kilt an' the music's lilt
Mak some o' the lads feel grand.
But fa enjoys sic a helluva noise
As ye get fan the band cuts loose?
It perforates yer ear-drums, but
It gets ye oot o' the hoose.

It's nae that he's a saftie,
But a pipe band's nae sae crafty –
On a windy day it's draughty,
But it gets ye oot o' the hoose.

We love an evenin's gamblin' – oor confidence abounds.
I play roulette,
I bet and bet,
I lose ten thousand pounds.
Then my mortgage goes and the bank foreclose –
They winna tak nae excuse.
There's one sure thing aboot gamblin' – it
Can get ye oot o' yer hoose.

The North-East Oscars   (AG)

P.A. Voice: And now we are going over to the show business awards for the Grampian area. Over now to meet the compere for the evening, the super new Country and Western star, Aberdeen's answer to George Hamilton IV – Harry Yorston V.

(Enter a Country and Western singer carrying a guitar.)

Harry: Ladies and gentlemen. Fit aboot it a' then? Magic is't, eh? It's nae real is't? It's mental this eh? The hale o' Aiberdeen's show business is here the nicht. Bill Tough, the doorman at the Beach Ballroom. Daisy Duguid, the Alexander Brothers' landlady. Isla St. Clair's postie. The lead drummer in the Orpheus Choir. Mrs. Oslena Stott's ghost writer. In her case, that's the Holy Ghost!

We're a' here the nicht, eh? A real nicht o' glamour this, eh? Ken fit I mean, eh, eh? An' fa's in charge o' the hale thing? The boy! The loon fae Heatheryfold. Wi' naethin' gan for me but my talent. Ye maybe winna believe this, but six months ago, I was naethin'. It is hard to believe, is't? But straight up, six months ago, I wis at the bottom o' the heap. I wis! A newly qualified solicitor, through the day, and at nicht, buskin' ootside the Grand Central. An' then, I brought oot my first Country and Western record. *She Wears a Yellow Ribbon But it's Got a Funny Smell 'Cos She Works in Claben.*

An' now, it's a' happenin' for me. A Golden Disc – at The Other Record Shop. Top o' the bill at Crazy Daisy's. My ain pad in Claremont St. And this wik, my very first drug offence. Probation fae Sheriff Russell. I'm really ower the moon aboot it. Ken fit I mean? Really magic. And here I am the nicht, and I've got here in my hand, the nominations for the best musical comedy – Hall Russell's daein' *Show Boat*. The Dons' Supporters Club daein' *Pal Joey*. But the winner, the winner for the best musical comedy in the North-East – Haddo Hoose daein' *Verdi's Requiem*. I didna see it mysel, but I believe it wis a good laugh.

The next prize is gan tae be handed ower by a gentleman, who earlier this evening won the award for best director: David Welch, Director of Links and Parks. And the prize that David's gan tae hand ower, is the award for the best comedy T.V. programme. And the nominations for the best comedy programme: *Police News, Open University Physics,* but the winner, of the best comedy programme – God Almichty . . . *Reflections*!

Reflections Doric word for *Late Call*

The Ashvale

Tune: The Ashgrove.

Off Holburn Street slightly
As kids we would gather nightly
At a chip shop unsightly,
'Twas called the Ashvale.
Supreme amongst chippers
When we were but nippers,
Aberdonians and Glasgow trippers
Patronised the Ashvale.

Oh! oft have I stood in
A queue for a mealy puddin'
They were something with which you couldn't
Find one single fault.
I've never seen ony
White puddin's as bonny –
Nae wonder Egan Ronay
Approved the Ashvale.

In the 50's big Rhona,
The wife of the owner,
My God! what a prima donna,
She ruled the Ashvale.
A powerful figure,
She wielded with vigour
A large bottle of vinegar
As she dished oot the chips.

Is my recollection
Obscured by affection?
Were the chips not perfection
Sold at the Ashvale?
Peeled with a blunt scraper,
Deep fried in a cloud of vapour,
Then wrapped in the evening paper
Or the *News of the World.*

Courting couples were rife there
I proposed to my wife there,
The decision of my life there
Outside the Ashvale.
I'd met her on Sunday,
I'd phoned her on Monday,
That evening we rendez-
Voused at the Ashvale.

But it's gone now – what folly!
Like the Playhouse and Andrew Collie.
These are blows to the quali-
Ty of North-East life.
This chipper that we went til –
I may be too sentimental,
But I'm sad that a continental
Cairry oot is now there.

Each year our rare species
Of chip-shops decreases,
And the latest of these is
The matchless Ashvale.
One of God's masterpieces –
Farewell the Ashvale.

Desert Island Discs

We hear the tune Sleepy Lagoon, *followed by a BBC voice announcing* Desert Island Discs. *The stage is lit to reveal Roy Plomley and a man wearing a cap.*

R.P.   How do you do, ladies and gentlemen. Our castaway this week is one of Britain's greatest ever sportsmen; he is quite simply the champion bowler of Auchnagatt, Mr. Sandy Thomson. Mr. Thomson ...

S.T.   Aye.

R.P.   Could we begin at the beginning?

S.T.   Aye.

R.P.   Were you one of a large family?

S.T.   Oh, very large sir. They were a' ower six feet bar me.

R.P.   Now your father also was a great bowler?

S.T.   Aye wis he, aye.

R.P.   What was your relationship with your father?

S.T.   I was his son.

R.P.   And your mother? How do you remember her?

S.T.   I ties a knot in my hunky.

R.P.   Now, how would you cope on your desert island? Would you find your own food? No supermarkets there!

S.T.   Oh, but there's nae supermarkets in Auchnagatt either. In fact, there's just naethin' in Auchnagatt. If ye can survive in Auchnagatt, ye can survive onywye.

R.P.   Now, if you could take one book with you, not the Bible or Shakespeare ...

S.T.   Oh, certainly nae the Bible or Shakespeare. Fit kind o' feel gype would tak' the Bible or Shakespeare?

R.P.   Well, which book would you take?

S.T. Oh, it would be a toss up between Jack Webster's *History of the Dons* and *The Kama Sutra* ... Here noo, fit aboot my records? I get eight records, ye ken.

R.P. Oh, I'm so sorry, I was forgetting. What would your first choice of record be?

S.T. Well, I think it would be *Fite Christmas*. Sung by Bing Crosby or Robbie Shepherd. Well, a' that stuff about the sna' comin' doon – it would just fair mind me o' a summer's day in Auchnagatt.

R.P. Well, I'm sorry, we've looked under F and we don't seem to have *Fite Christmas*.

S.T. Oh well, in that case, I'll just hae Dame Janet Baker singing *The Muckin' o' Geordie's Byre*.

R.P. Well, no problems there. Well now, could we get back to your bowling achievements. Now I understand that you have won the bowling championship of Auchnagatt each year for the past four years?

S.T. Aye hiv I, aye hiv I.

R.P. An achievement worthy to rank alongside that of Bjorn Borg?

S.T. Oh it's better than Bjorn Borg! He's never won the Auchnagatt Bowling Championships. Nae yet onywye, No, no.

R.P. Could we perhaps talk for a moment about one or two of the people you have defeated in the finals?

S.T. Oh, there was Horace Hunter the butcher. Oh, what a hard man was Horace Hunter. Oh, affa keen he was to get his revenge was Horace.

R.P. You had defeated him in some previous tournament?

S.T. Oh na, na, I was takin' up wi' his wife.

R.P. Could we move quickly on to last year?

S.T. Fairly that.

R.P. Last year, 1978.

S.T. Well now, last year was Father O'Reilly the local left-fitter. An' ye ken this, I played him in the final just a wik afore he got mairried.

R.P. Father O'Reilly?

S.T. Aye, aye. Ye ken this, he got a telegram fae the Pope! Wishin' him the best o' luck. That was for the bools final like, ken, nae for his nuptials.

R.P. Interesting. A telegram from the Pope?

S.T. Aye, Mind you, nae this Pope now. No, no. In fact it wisna the last Pope. God, 1978 was an affa bad year for Popes. It wisna great for barley, but it was waur for Popes.

R.P. I wonder if we could, perhaps change tack. . . . If you were to have one luxury with you on your desert island, what would it be?

S.T. A life-size model of Racquel Welch. I've got it at hame. I would just need tac blaw it up.

R.P. And would you try to escape?

S.T. I would not! Nae if I could get it richt blawn up.

R.P. And if you could have a second luxury?

S.T. A bicycle pump.

Kama Sutra N.E. farmers' good breeding guide.

Bad year for Popes Pope John Paul II's two predecessors had both died in that year.

Robbie Shepherd Disc jockey and Highland Games commentator; thus the North East's answer to both Jimmy Savile and David Coleman.

She's Wonderful

Tune: *They Say That Falling in Love is Wonderful.*

Steve: Jimmy Love's awa'.

Buff: He's awa', is he? How's Mrs. Love takin' it?

Steve: Oh, she's wonderful. Isn't she?

George: Wonderful. So they say.

They say that aul' Mrs. Love is 'wonderful'.
She's 'wonderful',
So they say.
Her man has gone up above – she's 'wonderful',
Just 'wonderful',
Folk'll tell you.
He tired o' married life, he
Has found a fancy wifie.
It's the wifie up the stair and they're living in
Sin.
That wye he's moved up above
And gi'en the shove
Tae Mrs. Love.
She's 'wonderful',
'Wonderful'.

Folk soon forget what she's been.
She's 'wonderful', she's 'wonderful'
Now he's gone.
She's coorse, malicious and mean,
But 'wonderful', she's 'wonderful'
Now he's left her.
Her tongue pulls folk tae pieces,
She's even misca'd Jesus.
She's the kind o' nesty wifie I canna stand,
And
Yet folk now say Mrs. Love is 'wonderful', 'wonderful',
Now he's away,
So they say.
Yes that ill-natured aul' besom's 'wonderful', 'wonderful',
Now that her gent's upped and went.

The American Visitor

Mr. Ellington, an American visiting Aberdeen, approaches a door and rings the bell. The door is opened to him by the householder, Mr. MacIntosh.

E.   Mr. MacIntosh?

M.   Aye.

E.   Mr. William MacIntosh?

M.   *(Suspiciously)* Aye?

E.   Mr. Billy MacIntosh?

M.   *(More suspiciously)* Aye.

E.   Well, hello Billy! My name is Chris Ellington and I'm over here from Los Angeles, California.

M.   Oh aye . . . Ye're nae a Mormon, are ye?

E.   No! I'm not a Mormon.

M.   No, I can see ye're nae a Mormon. Ye're nae smart enough for a Mormon. And if ye wis a Mormon, there'd be twa o' ye!

E.   That's right I'm not a Mormon.

M.   Ye're a Jehovah's Witness, then?

E.   No, I'm not a Jehovah's witness. Why if you must know, I am an agnostic.

M.   I kent ye wisna Church of Scotland onywye.

E.   No, I'm over here on vacation. Back home in L.A. I live right next door to your cousin Tommy MacIntosh and his very charming lady wife, Yvonne.

M.   Ohhh!

E.   And your cousin Tommy said if I were ever in Aberdeen, to be sure to look you up.

M. Well, my cousin had nae business. He's nae my real cousin onywye. He was born in 1943.

E. So?

M. Well, my uncle was taken prisoner at Dunkirk.

E. Tommy talks a lot about you.

M. Oh aye.

E. He says what a swell guy you are.

M. Oh aye.

E. A load of laughs.

M. Well, that's richt.

E. Last thanksgiving Tommy showed me some slides of you and your lovely lady wife, Elsie. Is Elsie at home this evening?

M. Aye.

E. Well, that's swell, I'm so looking forward to meeting Elsie.

M. Oh! Well ye canna! She's up the stair. In the jacuzzi. Wi' the rest o' the Woman's Guild.

E. It's been great visiting you in your lovely home. And experiencing your warm North-East hospitality. You certainly know how to make a guy feel welcome. I really have enjoyed our little chat.

M. Have ye? That's fine then, Cheerio.

E. And I look forward to telling Tommy that you and I, we finally met up. Have you got a message for Tommy?

M. Nuh.

E. Nothing at all?

M. Well, you can tell him, Broomhill Road was up the hale o' last year.

E. Sure will. Sure will.

M. And tell him we got the maple syrup he sent us for wir Christmas in 1963.

E. Sure will, yeah.

M. And ask him, if he got the shortbreid that we sent him for his Christmas in 1973.

E. Sure will. Yeah, yeah.

M. And tell him it's his shottie in 1983.

E. Sure will pass on that news to him the very next time I see him. We're scheduled to fly home three weeks Friday.

M. I'd better nae hud ye up then.

E. And if you ever come to California, you and Elsie must be our guests. We can show you a real good time. Parties by the pool. You can meet some of our Hollywood friends, Robert Redford and Jane Fonda . . .

M. Well, I wouldna hae ony objection tae that. The trouble is, Elsie's nae very sociable.

Auntie Flo's Tune

(Tune: Eine Kleine Nachtmusik – Mozart)

For her birthday I gave Auntie Flo
A Mozart record twenty years ago.
Nae lang efter I gave her it
It became her favourite,
She used to savour it;
Quite soon she had a love of Mozart,
Bocht mair stuff of Mozart,
Canna get enough of Mozart,
Now —
At the launderette
She will get
Funny looks when whistlin' a minuet,
And she's quite prepared tae
Hum concerti
When there's dirty
Dishes in the sink.

Hooverin' the lobby or the loo,
Flo plays a Mozart record.
Oot in the dryin' green, mind you,
She canna dae naething but sing.

While hingin' oot the washin',
Flo will sing with passion.
Her shrill coloratura
Reminds me of the Fuhrer.
It pierces the air,
An' folk get a scare,
As she sings Cosi Fan Tutte fan she's washin' doon the stair.

Oot at the baker's vannie
She listens tae her trannie.
The wifies that bide near her
First mocked her, now they cheer her.
They've become keen,
Now there's a scene –
There's Mozart sung in bingo halls a' ower Aiberdeen.

Then one day Flo married Joe McKay.
They'd a baby girlie by and by.
Ina – that was the name they chose,
Nae Marigold or Rose,
Nae Flow'ry names like those.
No, never: Ina McKay they called her
I know why they called her
That particular name:
They were anxious tae
Let her hae
A chance tae live her life in a Mozartian way.
So – a bloomin' shame –
The bairn's full name
Is Ina Kleine Nachtmusik McKay.

The A.G.M.

The Chairman of a prestigious Aberdeen Club is seated at the Committee table. He proceeds to conduct the A.G.M. addressing the members.

Ch.   Right gentlemen, I have much pleasure now in constituting this, the seventy-sixth Annual General Meeting of the Royal Commercial and Professional Club. Now, it's gone seven-thirty, the sooner we get the meeting started the sooner we'll get finished and through to the bar.

M.1.   Get on wi' it then! Get on wi' it! Get yer finger oot, min!

Ch.   Righto, Canon. Now gentlemen, we'll just take the agenda.

Item 1. Apologies for absence. Now, I've had an apology from Dr. Tommy Dewar. Tommy's on call this evening. So he can't be with us here. He has to be beside the telephone, through in the bar. Now, next item, Item 2. The minutes of the last meeting.

M.2.   Eh, Mr. Chairman. *(A very adenoidal voice)*

Ch.   Eh, yes Hebbie.

M.2.   I have much pleasure in moving the adoption of the minutes of the last meeting.

Ch.   Thank you very much indeed, and I know all the members will join me in wishing you all the best when you go into dock for your operation.

M.2.   Thank you, Mr. Chairman.

Ch.   What was it again, was it the adenoids or the hernia?

M.2.   Adenoids, Mr. Chairman, but I've had the operation last Bunday borning.

Ch.   Oh well, maybe ye should have tried the hernia. Right. Now, Item 3. The Annual Report.

M.3.   Mr. Chairman, I'm very pleased, yes I'm very pleased to propose, to propose that the Annual Report, the Annual Report be taken as read. Taken as read and approved, yes, approved.

Ch.   Thankyou Willie, for not only proposing it, but for seconding it as well.

Now, are there any questions on the report, gentlemen?

M.4. Mr. Chairman, your arrangements for the special darts night . . . Now, it was quite a good idea sir, inviting the world champion . . .

Ch. Thank you.

M.4. It's just a pity that this year it was Jocky Wilson.

Ch. Oh, come on now, Jocky didn't behave too badly. And the bar steward will be out of hospital soon.

M.4. It is a pity though that after knocking out the bar steward's teeth, which was probably fair enough, 'cos nobody likes him. Jocky then proceeded to remove his own teeth.

Ch. Ah well, Charlie, there's nothing in the club rules against removing your dentures. The rules only say that you have to wear a tie at all times. There's nothing about wearing your dentures. And Jocky was wearing a tie.

M.4. Aye, to haud up his briks.

Ch. Ah well, better up than doon. Right gentlemen, we'll move on now to the next item, the Annual Accounts.

M.5. Mr. Chairman, I would like to move the adoption of the annual accounts, please. 'Cos ye ken, I think it's terrific the wye it disna maitter hoo bad a year we've had, but the twa sides o' the balance sheet aye manages to come oot the same, div they?

Ch. Thank you professor. But we on the committee know that with an eagle eye like yours around, we have to be very careful when we're cook –when we're doing the books. Now, I don't suppose there are any questions about the accounts, gentlemen?

M.6. Mr. Chairman, What aboot the contract for the exterior painting work? I never got a chance tae pit in a price for that job!

Ch. Which contract?

M.6. The contract for painting the ootside o' the club premises.

Ch. Oh, that contract! You're not suggesting there was a fiddle?

M.6. No, I'm telling you there was a fiddle. And another thing Mr. Chairman, fit aboot the bandits, eh? This must be the only club in the hale world where the bandits make a loss. It's ridiculous. I mean, I pit in twa thoosand quid tae that machines masel.

Ch. Oh, come on now Andy, two thousand quid?

M.6. Aye, twa thoosand, I've got proof. 'Cos the money I pits in tae the bandits, I pits through my ain books as casual labour. So there's definitely dishonesty somewye.

Ch. Well gentlemen, I think you'll agree that's the kind of question that should be raised at an A.G.M. Thankyou very much Andy, for asking it. Any other questions now, gentlemen? No? Well, we'll move on to the last item, our old friend A.O.C.B. Almost off to commence boozing. Ha ha ha ha. Oh, I tell a lie, I tell a lie, I've missed Item 5. The election of office bearers. Can we have nominations for the post of Chairman of the Club?

M.7. Mr. Chairman, as my many friends in this club know, sir, I'm not given to flattery or sycophancy . . .

Ch. Hold on, I know the voice but I can't quite see, it's Jack Fraser. Where are you Jack?

M.7. I'm lying on the floor. Mr. Chairman.

Ch. Why are you on the floor, Jack?

M.7. I'm drunk, Mr. Chairman.

Ch. All right, Jack, the club rules specifically permit me to accept a nomination from the floor. Ha ha ha ha ha. You carry on, Jack.

M.7. Mr. Chairman, I have much pleasure in nominating you to serve a further term as Chairman of this club.

Ch. Thank you very much indeed. Would you care to make a statement in support of your nomination?

M.7. Most certainly sir, because I consider that throughout the past year, you have carried out you duties impecc - impy - impecci . . . I'm very sorry, Mr. Chairman, I can't read your writing!

The Mossat Shop

Tune: *The Muppet Show.*

Turn right, then left, past Alford,
Go on five miles, then stop.
The crowds of folk will tell you
That you've found the Mossat Shop.

It's a unique phenomenon,
Folk come from miles away;
Shop there, you won't regret it,
Anything you want you'll get it
At the Mossat Shop today.

A book on psycho-analysis,
A packet of cake-mix,
A pair o' 'lastic galluses
For huddin' up yer briks.

The range of stuff's tremendous,
All carefully on display;
There's fire-side rugs and fenders,
Ladies' and gents' suspenders
At the Mossat Shop today.

Photograph of Denis Healey,
Portrait of Dorian Gray,
A jar o' bramble jeely,
Deep frozen mince an' mealie
At the Mossat Shop today.

There's ornaments nae handy –
It's the busts that I like best;
There's a little bust of Gandhi
An' a big bust of Mae West.

A pair o' briks wi' patches,
Four wheels for a Ford coupé,
A box o' safety matches,
A wig like Maggie Thatcher's
At the Mossat Shop today.

A handbag for yer Auntie,
An instant cheese soufflé;
Some kiddies' gifts fae Sunty,
A Coronation chunty
At the Mossat Shop today.

This versatile emporium –
What treasures lie inside!
At mid-day or at 4 a.m.
Its doors are open wide.

Anything for which you hanker –
You only have to say:
A mango from Sri Lanka,
A needle or an anchor
At the Mossat Shop today.

And as for Marks and Spencer,
They're leaving Aberdeen.
They've made a frank admission –
Can't stand the competition
From the Mossat Shop today.

Nae shoppie could be classier,
It attracts the classy dames:
Princess Margaret bought a brassiere
When up for the Lonach Games.

Face-cream by Elizabeth Arden,
A case of Beaujolais,
Couture by Pierre Cardin,
Dung fae the Beechgrove Garden
At the Mossat Shop today.

Alka-Seltzer for your tummy,
First folio Shakespeare play;
You'll get a baby's dummy,
A fur coat for its Mummy.
The Harrods of Kildrummy –
That's the Mossat Shop today.

It's the most sensational,
        inspirational,
        unrepeatable,
        quite unbeatable –
It's the one and only Mossat Shop.

Santa's Phone Call

A man wearing a Santa Claus hat is speaking into an ancient telephone with a separate ear-piece.

Hello, hello. Is that Balmoral Castle? This is the Toy Shop, Ballater here. Santy Claus spikkin'! Could I speak to the Princess of Wales, please? Oh, it's yersel'. Oh very nice, foo are ye? God, fit a job I've hid gettin' through tae ye. Dis yer mither-in-law ken she's nae in the book? Ken this, I tried under Q, I tried under E.R., H.M. Nae sign o' her at a'. Then I tried under Balmoral, and I got a boardin' hoose in Great Western Road.

An' foo's he gettin' on, the wee man? Are ye managin' tae get yer sleep wi' him? My God yer lucky. Fit a job we had wi' oor aul'est . . . Oor aul'est. No, no, wir first born. No, no, nae Alice, aul'est. Mind you, her name *is* Alice, an' Alice jist aboot drove us up the wa'. By the time she wis on tae solids, I wis on tae liquids. Weel, Alice is twenty-two noo an' she was married last wik, an' fit a great affair it wis. Oh a great affair, a big do. It wisna as big as yours, ye ken, but I tell ye it wis the biggest do they've ever hid in the Kettledrum Tearoom in Ballater.

Fit's that? Oh, I'm sorry, I thought I had mentioned it tae ye. This is Santy spikkin' . . . Santy . . . No, no, nae Sandy, Santy. Mind you, my name is Sandy, Sandy Thomson, I used tae be the convener o' the Oldmeldrum Sports. That wis until I got the seck, like. Aye . . . Fit for? Weel last year the committee decided they wid just get a local celebrity tae open the sports, ye see, and they telt me tae fix up the Auchterturra dominie. Weel God, I didna hear them richt, and instead o' gettin' the Auchterturra dominie, I got the Ayatollah Khomeni. An' fit a weet blanket he turned oot tae be. He didna drink, he didna smoke, an' fan we tried tae pair him aff wi' the beauty queen, oh, he fair took the huff. He said she should be wearin' a veil. Mind you, if you saw oor beauty queen, I think he wis maybe richt.

Noo, fit wid he like for his Christmas, the loon? Fit aboot a pair o' fitba' beets? Beets, BEETS. B-O-O-T-S, BEETS. Weel I ken that, but he'll surely grow intae them. Weel I'll tell ye fit I've got. It's something very suitable. It's oor ain special line in soft toys, and it is, a cuddly futret. A futret. Div ye nae ken fit a futret is? FUTRET. F-E-R-R-E-T, FUTRET. Now cuddly futrets is exclusive tae the Toy Shop, Ballater. We get them specially made up, by a wee wifie, in Hong Kong. Oh, an' fit a job I hid explainin' tae *her* fit a futret is. Ye wid like a futret? Oh we'll fairly manage ye a futret. Noo fit size o' a futret wid ye like? We've got a dinkie futret, a mini futret, a life-size futret, a jumbo-futret or a mega-futret. Ye'd like a jumbo-futret? No, it disna hae a trunk. No, it's got a string that ye pull, an' it sings *Run, Rabbit, Run*. Weel fit else div ye expect a futret tae sing? Now is there onythin' else the loon wid like? Fit aboot a rubber Duke . . . for his bath? A duke. No, no, nae that kinda Duke. D-U-C-K, DUKE. A quack quack

duke. Like Donald Duke. Donald Duke. He's a freen' o' Mickey Moose ...
MOOSE ... M-O-U-S-E. MOOSE. God, div ye nae understan' English,
lassie?

Fit's 'at? Ye'd like twa dukes. Fairly that, we'll fairly manage ye twa dukes. Aye,
ye can ca' them fit ye like. Kent an' Gloucester? Please yersel'. Fit's 'at, No, no,
I'm sorry, I couldna come doon yer lum wi' them. No, we dinna dae deliveries
oot o' Ballater. Could ye maybe come in by yersel' the morn's mornin' an' pick
them up? That's fine. Wait till I see if the wife'll be here. Beldie, the Princess o'
Wales is comin' in the morn's mornin' for a jumbo futret an' twa rubber dukes.
Will you be here? Aye Beldie says she'll be here, 'at's fine, so you come in the
morn's mornin' an' we'll hae a'thing ready for ye. We'll hae a parcel made up
for ye, an' a gift cairdy made oot wi' the loon's name. Now, fit's the loon's name
tae pit on the gift cairdy? William, Arthur, Philip, Louis ... God, fit a hillock o'
names. I jist hope the day *he* gets mairried, *his* wife gets them in the richt
order.

'THAT'S FAR A' THE MONEY WENT'

There wisna muckle change oot o' three million quid. Three million quid was fit the Cooncil spent. That's fit the Coon-cil went and did, but far the hell his the money a' went? We're nae sayin' there's been blunderin', but a' body's been wonderin', Far the hell his the money a' went? Total reinforcement of the load bearing walls; That's far a' the money went. The Den-burn diverted thro' the Par-terre stalls; That's far a' the

money went. There's an ul-tra modern fleer got an an—ti static screed.There's a stereophonic amplifier Tae

TO CODA LAST TIME

waken up the deid, There's a brandnew safety curtain Adver—tisin' potted heid; That's far a' the

money went. We're nae sayin'there's bin blunderin', But a body's been wonderin', Far the hell has the

D.S

money a' went? money a' went? There's a

CODA

three piece suite in Jimmy Donald's front room That's far a'the money went!
(spoken)

135

That's Far A' the Money Went

There wisna muckle change oot o' three million quid.
Three million quid wis fit the Cooncil spent.
That's fit the Cooncil went an' did,
But far the hell his the money a' went?

Chorus

We're nae sayin' there's been blunderin',
But a'body's been wonderin',
Far the hell his the money a' went?

Total reinforcement of the load-bearing walls –
That's far a' the money went.
The Denburn diverted through the Parterre stalls –
That's far a' the money went.
There's an ultra-modern fleer
That's got an anti-static screed,
There's a stereophonic amplifier
Tae waken up the deid,
There's a brand new safety curtain
Advertisin' potted heid –
That's far a' the money went.

Facilities for the artists –oh! the hale rigmarole –
That's far a' the money went.
Every ither toilet has a toilet roll –
That's far a' the money went.
There's a lever that ye pull
That maks the stage ging up and doon.
There's a button that ye press
That maks the stage ging roon' an' roon',
They can even gie ye water
If ye're daein' *Brigadoon* –
That's far a' the money went.

And remember, if ye think there's been a gaff,
The capital investment has saved on staff:
The hale place is worked by a mannie ca'd Dod
Wi' a silicone chip in Victoria Road.

A' the new equipment is specialised –
That's far a' the money went.
Even Dod's kettle is computerised –
That's far a' the money went.
There's five hundred spotlights
On a cast-iron boom,
There's a closed circuit cam'ra
Wi' a telescopic zoom,
There's a three piece suite
In Jimmy Donald's front room –
That's far a' the money went.

There wisna muckle change In fact there wisna ony change. The refurbishment of His Majesty's Theatre which was completed in 1982 and which this song celebrates, cost £3.5m

Jimmy Donald Theatre Director (i.e. heid bummer) of His Majesty's, nephew of Dick (q.v.)

This is Your Life   (AG)

Eamonn Andrews (Buff) appears through the curtains carrying a big red book.

E.A. Hello, good evening. I'm speaking to you from His Majesty's Theatre, Aberdeen. And the man I'm looking for tonight is with the party from Aberdeen Football Club. He and his team-mates thought that they were coming to the theatre to see Scottish Ballet doing *The Nutcracker*. They thought a nutcracker was a kick in the goolies from Willie Miller. Be that as it may, tonight, Willie Miller, World Cup star, captain of the finest football club in Merkland Road, THIS IS YOUR LIFE.

(The curtains open to reveal a life-size cut-out figure of Willie Miller in football gear.)

E.A. Yes, Willie, this is your life. And the first to pay tribute to you tonight is Mr William Darkness, President of the SFA, a man dedicated to Scottish football as a whole, with no allegiance to any particular Club.

(Enter Mr. Darkness in Rangers clobber.)

E.A. Mr. Darkness, what do you admire about Willie Miller?

W.D. He's a wonderful example to the youth of Aberdeen. They a' model themselves on 'im. I've noticed since I've come up here. Every wee boy you meet in the street has got a wee black moustache.

E.A. Yes, and of course, Willie is a national figure.

W.D. Oh yes, Willie has appeared in the Scottish Team, the Scottish League Team and the notebook of every referee in Scotland.

E.A. Not that Willie is a dirty player. And Aberdeen are a clean team.

W.D. Oh aye. But the cleanest team in Scotland is Glasgow Rangers.

E.A. Rangers?

W.D. They must be. They've had mair early baths than onybody else.

E.A. Thankyou, Willie Darkness. *(Exit Willie Darkness)* But it is to Aberdeen Football Club that we must go for someone who knows you really well – the Chairman of the Club, Mr. Dick Donald. You thought at this moment Mr. Donald was, as usual, at Pittodrie counting the money, but at great expense we've transported him in a No. 1 bus along King Street,

Union Street, Union Terrace and here he is, Aberdeen Chairman, Mr. Dick Donald. *(Enter Dick Donald a respectable looking gentleman wearing glasses and a smartish hat)* Mr. Donald, what is your first memory of Willie Miller?

D.D. Fa?

E.A. The Captain of the Club.

D.D. Martin Buchan?

E.A. No, Willie Miller. Surely the Manager told you.

D.D. Ally McLeod never tells me naethin! We should never have got rid of Eddie Turnbull.

E.A. Mr. Donald. We're doing *This is Your Life, Willie Miller.* I'm Eamonn–

D.D. You're in show business. You're one of us. Here's a free pass for the Majestic.

E.A. Mr. Donald, I don't belong to Aberdeen, but I know the Majestic is closed.

D.D. Is it? Is it? Naebody tells me naething. I only ging tae the Grand Central.

E.A. The Grand Central is closed also.

D.D. Is it? I wis in there last Friday. I thocht there wisna mony folk in.

E.A. Getting back to football, Mr. Donald, we were talking about Martin Buchan.

D.D. Fa?

E.A. Martin Buchan. Went to Manchester United.

D.D. Did he?

E.A. Yes. Big transfer fee.

D.D. Oh, that Martin Buchan!

E.A. £125,000.

D.D. One hundred and twenty-six thousand pounds sixty-five pence plus VAT.

E.A. And of course, your own son Ian went to Manchester United.

D.D. Did he? I thocht I hadna seen him in the hoose for a while.

E.A. Mr. Donald, I'm surprised that as Chairman you don't sport the Club colours.

D.D. I've got my scarf wi' me, though *(He produces a black and gold scarf.)*

E.A. Aberdeen don't play in black and gold anymore. They play in all red now.

D.D. Div they? Naebody telt me. Gee whiz, that means every Setterday efterneen I'm cheerin' the wrang team!

E.A. Thankyou, Dick Donald. *(Exit Dick Donald.)*
Now Willie, you may not be aware who your greatest fan is, but here he is, all the way from Sharnydubs, Jockie Gillanders. *(Enter Jocky, an agricultural figure wearing bunnet, red galluses and scarf)*
Now Jockie, this year's Cup Final, Aberdeen 4, Rangers 1., after extra time, was a big day for Willie. It was a big day for you too?

J.G. And how, Eamonn. The Scottish Cup final, 1982, me and some o' the boys went doon tae Hampden in style, on Dod Walker's tractor, wi' the bogie ahint.

E.A. It's a long way to go on a tractor.

J.G. Oh, it's a lang wye tae go. So tae gie oorsels time, we set off early, jist as soon as we got the kye milkit at fower o' clock in the mornin', on the Wednesday. The wik afore.

E.A. The week before the final?

J.G. The wik afore the semi-final.

E.A. What sort of speed did you go at?

J.G. Oh, a helluva lick! Weel ye ken The Tyrebagger Eamonn? Weel, goin' doon the Tyrie, we had that tractor up tae damn near fifteen mile an 'oor. But then we had tae slow doon, gan up the Cairn-o'-Mount.

E.A. The Cairn-o'-Mount?

140

J.G. Aye.

E.A. That's a strange way to go?

J.G. Ah well, but we had tae pick up the Finzean branch o' the Dons' Supporters Club, at the Brig-o'-Feugh. Bill Strachan his name is. Fae Straun.

E.A. Bill Strachan from Straun?

J.G. Aye, or is it Bill Straun fae Strachan? I can never mind. Course they spik an affa queer wye doon aboot Finzean, ye see. It's a lot nearer England, of course.

E.A. Now, you had difficulty getting up the Cairn-o'-Mount?

J.G. Aye, the radiator biled ower, so we jist made a cup o' coffee.

E.A. Did you get to Hampden on time?

J.G. No, we missed the match, but they verra kindly put on half an 'oor's extra time for us and saved up twa or three goals.

E.A. Thank you very much, Jocky Gillanders. Thankyou. *(Exit Jocky)*
Earlier this year, Willie, your play in the World Cup won you many new admirers all over the world, even in Italy, home of the ultimate winners. And one man in the Vatican became a devoted fan. Listen to this voice.

P. *(Voice over P.A.)* Hello Villie. Last night in ze Vatican after vespers, I vos plyink snooker, with one of ze cardinals, Hurricane Guillianotti. Do you remember, Hurricane, Villie? Durink ze world cup, he had a part-time jobbie, sellink ice-cream, out of ze Pope-mobile.

E.A. Yes, Willie, you haven't seen him since the Brazil match, when he ran on to the pitch and kissed the penalty spot. Your number one fan in the Vatican. Pope John Paul II *(Enter the Pope)*

E.A. Your Holiness. Do you have a story about Willie?

P. Ah yes. Wan has just come to mind .... When I met Villie, I askit him, where in Scotland would I find, the biggest collection of sinners. And here I am. Fit like?

E.A. Do you watch Willie on television?

141

P.   Oh yes.

E.A.   Of course, reception of Scottish programmes isn't good in Italy.

P.   In some parts of Italy. But in the Vatican – How you say in Scoatlan'?
        'The deil looks efter his ain.' And our favourite programme is *Sportscene*.
        Even though that Archie MacPherson is a rotten Rangers
        supporter.

E.A.   Surely my colleague Archie is always neutral?

P.   No. He must be an Orangeman. Look at the colour of his hair! Mind
        you, now that *Sportscene* has been movit to Sunday, I cannot see eet,
        because I have awkward sheefts. But I am not complainink, because I
        get double time.

E.A.   How about yourself, your Holiness. Have you ever played football?

P.   Only once, and I vos not good. They put me at outside right. And I'm a
        natural left-footer

E.A.   Thank you Pope John Paul II *(Exit the Pope)* Finally, Willie, quite a
        number of your fans followed you to Spain this summer, and some of
        them haven't made it home yet. If you look over there, you'll see how
        they're managing.

(One of them, in tartan scarf and Spanish Sombrero is at the piano, playing Lady of Spain. *He is joined by the two others, and all three begin to sing.)*

We are three Scottish supporters.
Far is the pilot that brought us?
The eejit's went hame and forgot us–
We've been stuck here since July.

Oor package deal seemed quite thrifty.
I thocht the agent wis shifty:
Four weeks all found for six-fifty,
So we'd a foosty hotel.

The staff wis a' Chiefs an' nae Injuns;
The rooms either bad yins or grim yins
We shared een wi' six Argentinians
They were na friendly at a'.

The fitba' we jist couldna squeeze in.
The late kick-aff time wis the reason
By kick-aff time we wis ayc bleezin' –
We never saw Scotland play.

The weather has been getting hotter.
Last nicht we drank unbiled water.
This mornin' – oh! fit a sotter:
A'body needin' the loo;
I wis the last in the queue.

That's bad enough, but there's mair:
The chef's lyin' deid doon the stair,
And he was a legionnaire.
Leave yer paella alane,
We'll get a bus or a train,
Let's get tae hell oot o' Spain – Olé!

Willie Miller By common consent, particularly at Ibrox and Parkhead, the world's greatest footballer ever.

Merkland Road The street leading to Pittodrie stadium (N.E. corruption of 'the road to Mecca').

Dick Donald Chairman of Aberdeen Football Club. Uncle of Jimmy (q.v.)

Under the Carpet

Mr. Wallace is discovered kneeling on the floor with a hammer in his hand. He sings as he works. He pulls an old newspaper from beneath the carpet.

W. Fit's this? An aul' foostie newspaper underneath the carpet? I wonder foo auld this paper would be then?

(Enter Mr Taylor)

T. Aye, aye, Mohammed. Ye're facin' the wrong wye, min! Mecca's that wye!

W. Eh?

T. Mecca's East. Ower past Balnagask.

W. Fit ye spikkin' aboot Mr. Taylor?

T. Is that yer prayer mat ye're rollin' up?

W. No, I'm just fixin' doon the carpet. We've jist hid the hoose re-wired. And I found this auld foostie newspaper in ablow it.

T. An auld newspaper in ablow yer carpet? 'At's an antique that. You should send that tae Arthur Negus.

W. Fa?

T. Arthur Negus. He's an expert.

W. An expert on aul' papers? Ken 'is, Mr. Taylor, this paper must be 1962. 'Cos that's fan the carpet went doon.

T. Oh.

W. Aye.

T. Weel, ye ken this, when I came in here, and saw you looking at a 1962 paper, ye ken fit I thought?

W. No . . .

T. I thought – your delivery loon must be even slower than oors.

W. But we dinna get oor paper delivered. I get it fae **R.S. McColl** on the wye hame at tea-time. And I sometimes gets a packet o' Maltesers. Wid ye like a Malteser?

T. No thanks.

W. Aye we ta'en ower that carpet in 1962 when we bought the hoose. It cost us a hunner an' twenty quid.

T. You got a bargain, didn't ye!

W. Eh?

T. A hoose like this for a hunner and twenty quid! I'd hae pit it nearer two hunner.

W. No, no. No, no. The carpet. Ye see, it was the carpet that cost a hunner an' twenty quid. We ta'en it ower as new.

T. As new!

W. As new . . . Hey look fit was on at the picters in they days, eh? The Astoria. Mind the Astoria?

T. Aye, the Stoshie, the Stoshie.

W. *Brief Encounter* starring Celia Johnston and . . .

T. Frankie Howerd! Ha, ha!

W.   That's nae fit it says here … No, it was Trevor Howard.

T.   I *ken* it was Trevor Howard.

W.   A' richt. Nae need tae be nesty aboot it.

T.   *Brief Encounter*, eh? I saw that at the Astoria!

W.   Did ye?

T.   Aye. The back row of the back balcony, 2/3d wi' Bunty Jessiman.

W.   Bunty Jessiman, eh? Bunty Jessiman!

T.   Did you see it at the Astoria?

W.   No, I missed it. I mind saying to mysel', I'll wait till it comes back tae the Queen's.

T.   Ah, did ye see it at the Queen's?

W.   No, I missed it again. I was aff my work wi' a blin' lump. I mind saying tae mysel, I'll just wait till it comes back tae the Cinema Hoose.

T.   And … ?

W.   Well, ye'll never guess this Mr. Taylor.

T.   I will, I will. Ye missed it again?

W.   Fit wye did you ken? Aye, I missed it again. And then I missed it ten year later when it come tae the Theatre. It was at the Theatre ye ken! It was on a double bill wi' *Swedish Bedtime Frolics*.

T.   So are you sittin' there, tellin' me you've never seen *Brief Encounter*.

W.   Aye, I saw it last year on Grumpian. On a Sunday efterneen. Only, I missed the end o' it. 'Cos Mary switched it ower tae see *Rugby Special*. Fit happened at the end onywye.

T.   Well, Cardiff beat Swansea, 23-12. *(Pause)*

W.   He-he-he-he-he. At's good 'at! … No, no, fit happened at the end o' the picter?

T.   Well, I canna mind what happened at the end o' the picter. I canna mind naething aboot it. A' I can mind is Bunty Jessiman.

W. Ho-ho, Bunty Jessiman, eh? Bunty Jessiman. Did you really take Bunty Jessiman tae the picters?

T. Once. Just the once. It was the best two and threepence I ever spent in my hale life.

W. I'll bet it was! I'll bet it was! Did ye enjoy the picter?

T. I never seen the picter! But Bunty Jessiman!

W. Bunty Jessiman! . . . Fa did Bunty Jessiman finish up getting mairried til again?

T. Eddie Walker fae Sinclair Road . . . Or was it Eddie Sinclair fae Walker Road? No, it was Eddie Walker, it was Eddie Walker.

W. Aye.

T. He's deid now, Eddie. He died aboot five year ago.

W. Aye, aye, Eddie was a lot aul'er than Bunty of course. If Eddie had been alive the day, he would be . . . Ohhh . . . seventy-two. Course, Bunty got mairried again, ye ken.

T. Did she?

W. Aye, she mairried an aul'er man.

T. Aul'er than fa?

W. Aul'er than Eddie would have been if he'd been alive the day.

T. But if Eddie had been alive the day, she couldna hae mairried the ither mannie!

W. Oh *(He reflects on this)* If my Granda was alive the day, he would be a hunner an fourteen. What a wonderful aul' man he would be!

T. But he's nae alive the day!

W. No, no, he was killed at Gallipoli . . . And if my Grunny was alive the day, she would be a hunner and twenty. 'Cos she was aul'er than my Granda, fin they got mairried.

147

T. Fin they got mairried?

W. Aye, fin they got mairried ... and later on as weel.

T. My Granda *is* still alive.

W. Oh aye.

T. He's ninety-two! He come through baith wars.

W. Oh, he was lucky, wis he.

T. Nae really. He was a deserter in the first een. And an air-raid warden in the second.

W. Oh, but there was some air-raid wardens in a lot o' danger.

T. Nae in Lumphanan.

W. I think I met your Granda aince?

T. Yes, yes. In a long life, he has had the odd bad moment.

W. Oh? I'm sorry to hear that now. But foo's he keepin' onywye? Is he still playin' table tennis?

T. Oh aye, Well ye've got to keep going haven't ye?

W. Aye, aye.

T. 'Gather ye rose-buds while ye may. Old time is still a-flying.'

W. Shakespeare?

T. Robbie Burns. Robbie Burns. It has tae be. An' afore ye say it. If Robbie Burns was alive the day, he would be two hunner and twenty-three.

W. Two hunner and twenty three? ... Oh, but that's really aul' that! I mean, that's fantastic that, isn't it!

T. But he's nae alive the day! He died young Robbie, he was only thirty-seven.

W. Was he? Only thirty-seven eh? Only thirty-seven? Bloomin' shame! A young man. I mean, if he had lived his full span, ken? Three score years and ten. Foo aul's that, onywye?

T. Seventy.

W. Seventy. Seventy . . . A'richt then, ye dinna need tae get nesty aboot it. If he'd lived tae be seventy, foo aul' wid he be noo?

T. *(incredulous)* He would still be the same!

W. Oh no.

T. He would, of course he would!

W. Oh no, Mr. Taylor. If he'd lived to be seventy instead o' thirty-seven, that's another thirty-three years. Now, you see, Mr. Taylor, ye canna be the same age if you've lived another thirty-three years . . . He would be . . . two hunner and twenty-three plus thirty-three equals two hunner and fifty-six.

T. *(After consideration)* Aye, that would be richt. *(Pause)* Here, fan did you say that carpet went doon?

W. 1962. Just before we bought the hoose. April 1962.

T. So this paper should be 1962?

W. That's fit I telt ye.

T. But look at the date on't – 1942.

W. 1942! That means that carpet's been doon there since 1942! An' they telt us it was new in 1962. 'At's shockin' 'at! eh? Twenty year I've sat here thinkin' that's a new carpet. And now you tell me it's forty-year-aul'.

T. Weel dinna blame me, it's nae my fault! Fa did ye buy the hoose fae?

W. It was aul' Jockie Sutherland. Wid I hae a claim against him?

T. I shouldna think so. He's deid.

W. Is Jockie Sutherland deid?

T. Is Jockie Sutherland deid? I'll tell ye foo lang Jockie Sutherland's been deid. If Jockie was alive the day, he'd be even aul'er than Robbie Burns.

Foostie newspaper *The Sun*.

Expert on foostie newspapers Rupert Murdoch.

Edinburgh Castle

The year is 1137, and the scene is the Town Planning Department of the City of Edinburgh. The Director of Town Planning is making a phone call.

Hello, is that King Malcolm of Scotland? Good morning. Director of Town Planning here. Sorry to bother you, but I've got your application here for outline planning permission, and there are just one or two points I'd like to get cleared up. Now have I got this right? You're proposing to build some kind of castle, bang in the middle of Edinburgh, on top of that lump of rock overlooking Princes Street Gardens and Waverley Station. Now is that right? Because if it is, Your Majesty, you're away with the fairies. All these years of royal inbreeding must be catching up with you. No, no. No disrespect, Your Majesty, but I mean to say, a great monstrosity of a castle, sticking up like a sore thumb, directly opposite two of Scotland's finest natural treasures – British Home Stores and Marks and Spencer. It'll ruin the whole character of the city.

And I'll tell you this, you're going to have some fearful technical difficulties. I mean, that's solid volcanic rock there. How are you going to get a sewage pipe through it? Well, but as I understand it, Your Majesty, you're going to have a garrison of 500 troops there. What arrangements are you going to make for sewage? A chain of buckets? All the way down to the Forth? That's a lot of buckets. I mean to say, we are living in the twelfth century after all. The Environmental Health people just won't wear it. Environmental Health, Your Majesty. Used to be called the Sanitary Inspector, before the 1066 reorganisation.

Now, what else was I going to ask you? Sorry I'm a bit woozy this morning, but I was at the Watsonian Dinner last night. I saw your son there – the heir to the throne. But he's not a Watsonian. No. You couldn't get him into Watson's. Where did you get him in? Stewart's-Melville? Dear God. But he got kicked out of there, and he's in Borstal now. Oh, well, it's not as bad as Stewart's-Melville.

There's a word here on the plan I can't quite read. It looks like 'gun', but it can't be 'gun'. What's that? It *is* 'gun'? Every day at 1 o'clock, you propose to fire off a gun from the castle. What on earth for? To let people know what time it is? But there's a perfectly good clock on top of the North British Hotel. And I'll tell you this. If you're going to be firing off artillery from domestic premises, you've really got to watch it. Have you served notice on adjoining proprietors? 'Cos you've a guy down the road from you there in the Royal Mile – John Knox – a right bloody kill-joy, I can tell you. I don't know what he does for a living, but there's not an ounce of Christian charity about him.

Now, have you got an architect for this hare-brained scheme? I only ask,

because there's no name at the bottom of the plan. And in my experience that means you've got someone from the City Architect's department, to do a homer. You have? Who did you get exactly? The City Architect himself? Well, with him as your architect, you'll need a damn good contractor. Who have you got? Barratt's. And the best of British luck to you. Oh, no, I quite agree, their publicity is very good. Of course, they've got a helicopter, specially invented for them by Leonardo da Vinci. And they've opened a new European division. They've just built a tower, at Pisa. And from all accounts they haven't got it quite right.

Well, well, to get back to your application, it is very unusual. I mean, the kind of thing I usually deal with is – well, like the application I had yesterday, for a double lock-up in Corstorphine. Even that was tricky. I'd a helluva job finding a good reason to throw it out. It was quite attractive – pebble dash finish with an up and over door. Something like that would look quite nice on top of that rock. Or what about a nice wee factory, with plenty of concrete and galvanised steel? Or could you not put up an office block like everybody else? There's never any planning difficulty with that kind of thing.

Parents' Night

Mr. Turnbull, a teacher, is seated at his desk in his classroom. Mr. Christie, a parent, wearing a cloth cap, is examining specimens of class work on the wall. Mr. Turnbull glances at his watch impatiently.

T. Are there any parents I haven't seen yet? *(He turns to Mr. Christie)* I don't think I've spoken to you?

C. Oh, sorry, sorry.

T. Come away and sit ye down.

C. By jove, some o' that bairns can fairly draw, can't they, eh? It's hardly like a classroom this at a'.

T. Yes, some of the pupils have done good work.

C. Ye ken the een I like best? It's the drystane dyke, wi' the coo lookin' ower't. It's jist a topper, that. He jist seems tae hiv catched the expression on that coo's face. It's affa real, ken fit I mean?

T. Well, it should be. It's a photograph.

C. Oh, it's a photograph!

T. Yes.

C. It's nae a drawin'?

T. No, it's a photograph.

C. Well, it's nae a great photograph. It wid be affa good if it wis a drawin', but it's nae a great photograph. Funny business, that, intit?

T. I'm sorry, you are – ?

C. Christie o' Sharnydubs.

T. Oh yes. Hello, Mr. Christie. Now, it's Duncan that you're here about?

C. Aye, aye.

T. *(Looking at his register)* Here he is, Duncan Alexander Oliphant Christie.

C. That's him. That's him . . . God, I had forgotten aboot that third name, there, now that you mention it. That's fae his mither's side that, ye see.

T. Oh, his mother's an Oliphant?

C. Oh, she's huge! Oh aye. Fit a size o' a woman she is.

T. I don't think you and I have met before. You weren't at last year's parents' night?

C. No, no, I couldna manage the parents' nicht last year. No, that was the nicht I had to take Duncan to see the Police.

T. To see the Police! The sergeant at the station?

C. No, the pop group at the Capitol. And oh, fit a steer o' folk there wis! I lost my bunnet. In the stramash in the cloakroom. There wis a skinheid went awa' wi' it. Mind you, I didna blame him. It wis an affa nicht o' caul'. I think the tap o' his heid wis frostit. Ye get neeps like that, ye ken!

T. So, that's a new bunnet you have on tonight?

C. Oh, this is my second bunnet since that pop concert. I lost anither bunnet at Shakkin' Stevens.

T. Another skinhead?

C. No, no, but oh, fit a skinheids there wis at Shakkin' Stevens! Oh aye. Well, Duncan an' me wis up in the balcony, an' lookin' doon on the stalls, there wis rows o' them. Rows an' rows o' skinheids in the stalls. Ye ken fit they looked like?

T. A park o' neeps?

C. No, a box o' eggs.

T. Oh well, but it's very nice to meet you this year.

C. Oh, but it's nice to meet you. I've seen ye gan aboot of course. There wis ae day I wis twa ahin' ye in the queue at the bunk.

T. Oh yes.

C. Aye. Mphph. Did ye get your personal loan for your new car a' richt? I thocht the manager seemed affa sweirt. But I thocht yer salary wis good enough. And sae did a'body else I wis spikkin till aboot it. It wis jist a Toyota onywye ye wis sikkin', wisn't it?

T. Yes, a Toyota, we bought it from Walter Rattray's Garage. He's the Toyota and Honda agent.

C. Aye, aye, ye see, I'd never buy a Jap car, never buy a Jap car. On principle.

T. Did you have a bad experience in the war?

C. No, I just canna stick that Walter Rattray. Weel, weel, are ye settlin' in a' right? Good, good. Uh huh. Have ye got a hoose yet?

T. Yes, yes. We've bought the house at the corner of Garioch St.

C. Oh! nae Ythanbank? Wis't you that bocht Ythanbank? Ho ho ho ho. Forty-seven thoosand?

T. How do you know?

C. The minister telt me . . . Forty-seven thoosand for a packet o' trouble. Are the drains a' richt noo?

T. Well, nobody told us anything about the drains.

C. Well, they widna, wid they? But Bill Benzie, him that had the hoose afore you, he wis aye gan tae get that drains seen til. But the typhoid got him first. Weel, weel. But I'm nae here tae listen tae a' your tales o' woe aboot yer hoose. It's Duncan I'm here aboot. Foo is he gettin' on, the loon?

T.   Well, Duncan, yes. What can I tell you about Duncan? Well, Duncan's a character. He's a character. He's very active. Physically and verbally. He's highly extroverted. He's a very good example of what we educationalists call —

C.   A bloody nuisance.

T.   Well, that is one way to put it.

C.   That is the only wye tae put it! Oh, fit a handful he is, fit a devil he is. I dinna ken aboot you, but he connachs me! It's a' that leatherin' I gie him. Every night, ye ken! God! and some nichts he deserves it.

T.   Well, of course, as an enlightened educationalist, I don't like corporal punishment.

C.   Well, neither does Duncan! He disna like it at a'. So my advice tae you is – hud in wi' that scud, boy. And atween the pair o' us, we'll brak in the little bugger yet.

T.   Can I ask you this, Mr. Christie? Does Duncan spend a lot of time on his homework?

C.   Well, no, he disna ye see. He's aye scutterin' aboot the ferm at something else. Last nicht I says till him 'Duncan', I says, 'come awa' fae that bull . . . wi' the kitchen scissors. That's a job for the vet.' I says tae him, 'Have ye nae lessons tae dee. Have ye nae tables tae learn?'

T.   No, no, in the modern system, there is no place for the rote learning of multiplication tables.

C.   Nae tables! But fan I wis a loon at the school a' that ye did wis yer tables. But eence ye'd learned yer tables ye never forgot them. Richt up tae twelve times twelve is a hundred and thirty-two. I never forgot that, ye see.

T.   But twelve twelves is a hundred and forty-four. You've just demonstrated that the old method didn't work.

C.   Well, it's workit fine for me! 'Cos I sell my eggs by the gross.

T.   If we could get back to Duncan for a moment, Mr. Christie. Now, next year Duncan moves into the senior school, and under the Parents' Charter, you have a choice of schools you can put him to. Now, of the schools available, one is good for maths, one for English, one for science –

C.   Oh, no, no. We've made up oor minds aboot that. He's gan tae

Inverurie Academy.

T. For the maths?

C. No, he'll get his dinner fae his auntie. She's the jannie's bidie-in.

T. Now, you'll find in the senior school these days, there's no such thing as a streaming of pupils. In every class there are some very clever pupils. Some not so clever. Some not clever at all. And some –

C. Like Duncan. And fa will he get for a teacher fan he gings tae the big school? 'Cos he's aye likit you fine. For a' that you broke his thoomb ae day. Fan ye hit him wi' yer pointer. For forgettin' his milk money. I wouldna care, but it's me that supplies the milk!

T. Well, at least with me, Duncan knew where he stood.

C. Ootside the door maist the time. But for a' that he's aye said you were the best teacher in the school – at throwing that widden blackboard duster.

T. Yes, I don't often miss.

C. No, he wis jist sayin', last Tuesday, ye hit ae loon twice. First in the ee, and then on his airm.

T. Yes, John Eddie.

C. And dae ye ken fit they ca' him noo? Nelson Eddy!

T. Excuse me for mentioning this, Mr. Christie, but you look rather old to have a boy of eleven.

C. God, I'm only eighty-six, min.

T. Well, exactly. Presumably your wife's a lot younger.

C. Oh, but I'm nae mairried.

T. So who is Duncan's mother?

C. Well, that's Miss Oliphant, the housekeeper.

T. I see. Duncan is the housekeeper's boy and you're the father?

C. Well, that certainly is one possibility.

T. One possibility?

C. Aye. Well I ferm Sharnydubs wi' my brither, Jimmy. And Miss Oliphant, the housekeeper, has been a very good friend tae baith o' us.

T. And you *call* her Miss Oliphant?

C. Oh, aye. She's affa perjink. I think her name's Betty, but I've never been on first name terms wi' her. And neither has Jimmy.

T. But wouldn't you like to know if it's you or Jimmy that Duncan belongs to?

C. Well, we hiv kind o' half-wondered files. I mean, on Duncan's last birthday, I says tae Jimmy, 'Look here, Jimmy', I says, 'I'm nae spendin' a' that money on a new bike if I'm jist his uncle.'

T. Well, anyway, Duncan is Miss Oliphant's son, and I can take it that it's either you or Jimmy who's the father?

C. Oh, aye. She never gings oot. And we never hae visitors. Well, jist the minister fan he's on his rounds, like.

T. Well, I think we can rule him out. But you would like to know?

C. Oh, we'd like fine tae ken. An' maybe you're the man tae help us.

T. Me? How can I . . .

C. Well, fan Jimmy an' me wis at the school, my best subject wis sums and Jimmy's best subject wis spellin'. Now, fit's Duncan's best subject?

T. Well, it's Bible Study.

Capitol Former cinema in Aberdeen, now the venue for deafening pop concerts. Hence 'Capitol punishment'.

Stramash The stage in a public disturbance between a stooshie and a punch-up.

Toyota Second-hand Japanese banger assembled in Auchterturra.

Scud Acronym: Scud – Something for Curing Undisciplined Devils. The belt – a mild form of corporal punishment favoured by the more liberal Aberdeenshire dominies.

'DAYS HERE AND THERE'

♩ = 69 With resignation

I've got a pleasant job, Tho' there is na much o'a wage in't, I earn an honest bob, I

colla voce

am a travel a-gent. Far-ever folk want tae ging, I smile & I say, 'Oh sure. I've got the very thing. Now

here's a braw brochure. Oh! Washington or Bombay, I'll or-gan-ise your ho-li-day.'

brightly, but with a
(covetous air)

♩ = 76

I've got cli-ents_____ by the

thoo-san'_____, some are fly-in'_____, some are crui-sin'_____, I've a wif-ie fae the

159

there _____
o tempo

Days Here and There

Intro
I've got a pleasant job,
Though there isna much o' a wage in't,
But I earn an honest bob –
I am a travel agent.
Farever folk want tae ging,
I smile and I say, 'Oh, sure.
I've got the very thing.
Now here's a braw brochure –
Oh! Washington or Bombay
I'll organise your holiday.'

Verse
I've got clients by the thoosan' –
Some are flyin', some are cruisin'–
I've a wifie fae the Spital gan tae Italy by air,
But each fabulous vacation
Is a terrible frustration,
'Cos I have got a wife that jist likes days here and there.
I deal in the romantic,
So it nearly drives me frantic
Fan oor summer holidays are days here and there.

Chorus
Days here and there,
Days here and there,
Oor summer holidays are days here and there.

Tae widen her horizon
I says 'Let's be enterprisin'.
I'll fix a trip tae Spain –
A golfin' package wid be rare.
Imagine, jist the pair o's
Playin' wi' Seve Ballesteros.'
But it's puttin' at Pitlochry on oor days here and there.
Majorca and Ibiza –
I have never been to either,
For neither's ever figured in oor days here and there.

The Editor of *Leopard*,
Willie Milller, Robbie Shepherd –
I've fixed up a' their hol'days with considerable care,
And as Robbie's pitt'n' his kilt on
In the Acapulco Hilton,
I'll be pittin' on my anorak for days here and there.
There's an Inverurie banker
And he's half-wye tae Sri Lanka,
While we're at Inverurie on wir days here and there.

There's a couple, Jean and Sammy
Haein' a fortnicht in Miami.
The mannie in the bedroom next to them's a millionaire.
They're lovin' it in Florida,
But I'm nae further forrader,
I canna get my wife tae change fae days here and there.
Jean and Sam reach Buenos Aires
On the day we're in St. Cyrus –
My wife says it's her fav'rite of our days here and there.

I telt her, 'Fit a drag you are
I fancy Nicaragua.'
I've pit my Grandad there on his concessionary fare.
And Grannie's holiday is
Climbin' in the Himalayas,
But Scolty is oor high-spot on oor days here and there.
I fancy gan tae India,
But she winna gee her gingcr,
Though we sometimes hae a curry on wir days here and there.

I've got a scaffie who is
Travellin' widely in the U.S. –
This week it's Oklahoma, Maryland and Delaware.
Fan *he* gets tae Kentucky
I'll be daein' the sights o' Buckie.
Ken 'is – I'm in a state aboot gan days here and there.
Afghanistan is chancy,
But if that's the place you fancy,
I'm sure it's mair exciting than gan days here and there.

From the brochures I've a feelin'
I would really like New Zealan',
Or New Delhi, or New York – I think I'd like them even mair.
But the kind o' places *I* go
Are New Byth and New Pitsligo;
I canna get worked up aboot oor days here and there.
Well, ye winna get me ravin'
Aboot one day in Stonehaven,
Though it's probably the highlight of oor days here and there.

Oh, Africa is fab, we
Could hae twa wiks in Zimbabwe.
A concorde flight oot there would be a marvellous affair.
But the wife wid ging and spile it –
She'd be speirin' at the pilot,
'Div ye ever use this aeroplane for days here and there?'

Days here and there Exhaustive research has confirmed that this is the Aberdonian's commonest
form of holiday.

Leopard Magazine about wild life in Aberdeen; a survivor in the publishing jungle.

Scolty A challenging peak on Deeside never attempted by Hillary or Tensing.

Speirin' Descriptive of a blunt person making a sharp enquiry.

At the Airport

Mr. Taylor and Mr Wallace approach each other from opposite sides of the stage. Mr. Taylor is pushing an Aberdeen Airport trolley containing one small case. Mr. Wallace is laden down with luggage, cases in both hands, and carrying his passport between his teeth.

T.   Aye, aye, Biggles!

W.   Mmm . . . mmmm . . . mmm.

T.   You been parachuted in wi' this lot?

W.   Ayeeee . . . mmmm . . .

T.   Ye just got aff a plane?

W.   Mmmmmm . . . mmmm.

T.   Far have ye come fae?

W.   Ummmm . . . mmmm.

T.   Wait a minute, fit's this in yer mooth *(He relieves Mr Wallace of his passport)*

W.   That's my passport.

T.   Far have ye been wi' yer passport?

W.   I've been in London.

T.   In London! Wi' yer passport?

W.   Aye, wid ye like tae inspect it? Naebody else has asked for it.

T.   Oho, I like the photograph. Very nice photograph. Lord Snowdon, I presume?

W.   No, it's me.

T.   You just got aff the London plane an' a'?

W.   Aye, Mary an' me was doon seein' the daughter. Mary's aye there, but I was affa keen to get hame in time tae see the match this efterneen.

T. I see ye didna manage tae get a trolley.

W. No, I couldna get a trolley.

T. Aye, ye've tae be pretty sharp tae get a trolley. I just beat an aul' wifie tae this een. I mean, that's some luggage ye've got there!

W. Aye.

T. Have ye had that lot through the customs?

W. No. There's naebody stopped me.

T. They will at Bucksburn, boy. Ha ha ha ha.

W. Naw, they winna! I'm gan the back road tae Mastrick.

T. Ye're nae gan hame afore ye ging tae the match, are ye?

W. Aye.

T. Ye're needin' yer time!

W. Oh, I've plenty time. Look at the clock, it's half past twelve.

T. Half past twelve! That's the time in Reykjavik!

W. Reykjavik?

T. Capital of Botswana.

W. Oh.

T. No, no, capital of Iceland.

W. Iceland? So if the folk in Iceland want tae ken the time they phone up Aiberdeen Airport?

T. No, no. This is an *international* airport –

W. An international airport?

T. A' that clocks there – they tell ye the time in the different parts o' the world. Reykjavik, Toronto, Hong Kong. I mean, the wye the time is in Hong Kong, there's a Chinese waiter . . .

W. A Chinese waiter?

T A Chinese waiter, he has his denner in Hong Kong, he gets on a plane in Hong Kong, an' he's here in Aiberdeen in time for his breakfast.

W. Aye, the next mornin'.

T. The same mornin'.

W. The same mornin'?

T. The same mornin'. So he gets twa breakfasts an' twa denners the same day.

W. Oh, well, that proves it, dis it?

T. Proves fit?

W. Chinese food's nae very fillin'.

T. Did you enjoy the flight today?

W. Oh, no, no. I dinna like flyin'.

T. Oh, awa', it was a lovely flight that, a lovely smooth landing.

W. Oh no, I dinna like comin' doon. And I dinna like gan up either. The bittie in the middle is nae sae bad. I mean, the day, I wis just beginnin' tae relax, and then the captain gets on the loud speaker. He says he hopes we're having a very pleasant flight. Weel, I thocht it wis real nice o' him. 'Cos I dinna ken the bloke! And then he says, 'We're cruising,' he says, 'at six hunner mile an 'oor. At thirty thoosand feet'. Cruising! I had tae ging tae the cloakroom.

T. Ach, it wis a lovely day for flying, though. Rare view oot the windae.

W. Oh, no, I widna look oot the windae. It's ower near the ootside.

T. Awa', it's great lookin' oot the windae, min! Ye can see a' the toons on the wye up. Birmingham, Newcastle, Edinburgh, Turriff. Aye, it depends on the pilot. If he's had twa or three gins, he'll tak ye on a tour roond the Broch. Did ye get a drink yersel?

W. No, I didna get a drink. I think the drinks cam' roon fan I wis in the cloakroom. Mind you, I didna want a drink onywye. I made sure I wis bleezin' afore I got on the plane.

T. Ye got yer lunch though? Ye enjoyed that? Yer little plastic tray. Yer four courses and coffee. It's a' computerised that, ye ken. At no stage is that lunch touched by human hands.

W. Weel, I got it a' ower *my* fingers. I dinna like 'at plastic packeties. An' I got a' mixed up. I put salt in my coffee. I put salad cream on my aipple pie. Then the plastic fork broke. It skited my drum-stick intae my orange juice. It couped a'wye. Oh, fit a mess it wis! ken?

T. Ah, but I ken fit you did. You emptied the hale lot, carefully, intae the sick bag on the back o' the seat in front o' ye.

W. Weel, that's fit I meant tae dee. But the boy in front o's, he was wearin' an' anorak wi' a hood on't. Oh, he wisna pleased. I thocht there wis a funny side til't, but he didna see it at a'. It's affa the wye some folk never see a joke.

T. Come on now, get that stuff ontae this trolley. Dinna say I'm nae good tae ye! Now is that a' the luggage ye've got?

W. No, I lost een at Heathrow. I pit it doon fan I wis haein' a cup o' coffee – a little black casie, just like yours.

T. Yer executive case?

W. Aye, they're good that executive cases. I get a' my dirty shirts and hunkies intae mine.

T. Dirty shirts and hunkies in an executive case?

W. Aye!

T. And your jim-jams?

W. My Jim-jams an a'. When we wis in London, Mary bocht me a pair o' lovely Harlequin jim-jams.

T. And fit aboot yer socks?

W. No, nae my socks. I wis only in London a wik. I didna need tae change my socks.

T. But yer executive case is nae for yer washin'! See this case o' mine? This case contains – one reid an' white scarf, one rosette, one season ticket, and one hip flask.

W. Are you gan tae the match an' a'?

T. Na, na. I'm awa' for a cup o' tea wi' Racquel Welch.

W. Oh, ye'll be sorry tae miss the match!

T. Look, I'm nae missin' nae match. Me an' this case, we've been tae them a' – Gothenburg, Budapest. Hamburg. Wis you on ony o' that trips?

W. No, I wis just at Basil.

T. Basil?

W. Aye. The Cup-Winners' Cup Final at Basil.

T. But the Dons were na in that Cup Final.

W. Oh, I ken that, but I wis a' booked up afore they were knocked oot.

T. Fit aboot this efterneen, though? Are the Dons gan tae win the day? Are ye lookin' forward tae the match?

W. I dinna ken. I dinna ken. If they're gan tae win, I'm lookin' forward til't. But if they're gan tae lose, oh, I'm nae lookin' forward til't at a'.

T. And when, pray, do you expect to know if ye're lookin' forward til't?

W. Oh, when it's finished. Definitely, I'll ken then.

T. I'll tell ye this. If you wis in Hong Kong iv noo, ye'd ken if ye wis lookin' forward tae the match.

W. Fit wye?

T. Mind fit I telt ye aboot the clocks? In Hong Kong it's half past seven at nicht. The match is finished ower there.

W. Awa' ye go.

T. I'm tellin' ye. Three hours ago. In Hong Kong they ken the score a'ready. Well, I'm awa'. Straight tae Pittodrie. Dae ye wish ye wis as weel organised as me?

W. Here, wait a minute Mr. Taylor. That isna your case. Look that's the leg o' my Harlequin jim-jams. This is my case! You must've picked it up in the coffee shop at Heathrow.

T. Weel, far's my case?

W. Ye must hiv left it at Heathrow!

T. But my ticket for Pittodrie's in that case. It'll be awa' tae Hong Kong or somewye!

W. Dinna worry aboot it Mr. Taylor. The wye the time is in Hong Kong, ye'll get it back again yesterday!

Reykjavik Town to the north of, but not as cold as, Auchterturra.

Broch Prehistoric settlement, now known as Fraserburgh.

Bleezin' See plootered (*The By-Election.*)

Plastic Packeties Late twentieth century invention, designed to deny access to any desperately needed commodity, chiefly food and drink.

Couped a'wye Large scale.

Jim-jams Arabic garments removed during jing-bang (q.v.)

Racquel Welch Always among the first in the fantasy jing-bang of any red-blooded male (or even of Mr. Wallace)

Basil Faulty pronunciation of Basle.

Sweet Song

Tune: *The Rowan Tree.*

Oh, Rowntree, Oh, Rowntree,
Fruit Gums is what you mean to me.
The world's best confection'ry
Is made by Rowntree.
I knock back plates of After Eights
To finish my high tea.
Sweetmeat purvey'r beyond compare,
That's you, my Rowntree.
Oh, Rowntree.

Oh, Rowntree. Oh, Rowntree
I'm fond o' Liqu'rice All-sorts tae.
I like the een wi' the layers atween
And the coconut circle tae.
But I'm nae too keen on the plain black een,
Well, ye ken what liquorice can dae.
So, all in all, Liqu'rice Allsorts fall
Far short of Rowntree.

Black Magic chocs and Dairy Box
And orange-flavoured Aero blocks
I love the rest, but I think the best
Is a Kit Kat wi' my tea.
But a Polo mint wi' a holie in't,
When you've been oot on a spree,
Means the wife will not know you're half-cut,
All thanks to Rowntree.

But Rowntree, my Rowntree,
Here ends my love affair with thee.
When last night I saw my *avoirdupois*
It fairly frightened me.
So I went to see my ain G.P.,
Who advised against obesity,
So straight away, I decided tae
Cut doon my Rowntree.

Holie Non-fattening centre of a polo mint

169

The Moderator

Two ministers are discovered singing the last few lines of a well-known hymn. After the rather discordant 'Amen', one steps forward to speak.

Minister: My friends, what a great joy and pleasure it is for me this crisp September morning to be standing here, in Crathie Kirk, in the shadow of Balmoral Castle, listening to the sound of my own voice, as I introduce to you our preacher for the day – the Moderator of the General Assembly, himself a great missionary, the Reverend David Livingstone Eric Liddell Mary Slessor Archibald. David became a legend in his own life-time when, on being offered his first charge, that of New Pitsligo, he said to the then Moderator, 'New Pitsligo,' he said, 'stuff that for a caper.' And when the Moderator said 'Archibald, it's either New Pitsligo or damnation!.' David replied, 'I'll take New Pitsligo. I've been to Edinburgh before.' This, then, is the distinguished theologian who is our preacher today. Take it away, David.

(He makes way for the Moderator to address the congregation.)

Moderator: My dear friends, as I look around this crowded kirk, it fairly warms the heart and makes me feel at once proud and humble to see my presence here today has brought out such a large attendance – including yourself, your Majesty.

Now, as Moderator of the General Assembly, I am called upon to preach in many different parts of Scotland. And beyond. Now, what – does – this –mean? Well, it means, that wherever I go, I can use the same sermon. And that is very important you know, because time is very precious when you're the Moderator, 'cos you're only in the job for one year. It's exactly the same as being Miss World. Although there are some differences. I've never had a kiss from Eric Morley. Nor yet, have I had to parade in front of the General Assembly, in a pair o' dookers.

Be – that – as – it – may. My text this morning is, 'As ye shall sow, so shall ye reap.' So. So, that's my text, yes. A man gets out of this life that only which he puts into it. Well, my dear friends, I've put forty years into the kirk, and this is the year I'm takin' the hale lot oot! And that's why, ye know, although I've only been in the job for three months, me and the wife, on our travels, have already stayed at the New York Sheraton, the Calcutta Skean Dhu and a luxury wikkend at the Burnett Arms at Banchory.

That said, this wikkend at Balmoral, as Your Majesty's house guest, is the big one. What a super time I've had. Right from the moment I stepped off that Alexander's bus at your Majesty's road end. That was on Friday afternoon and I arrived in time for afternoon tea. Oh, what a lovely cup o' tea ye get at

Balmoral. Poured by her Majesty herself.

'Well now Moderator', she says, 'Will I be mother?' and then she looks at me, you know, and she says, 'Indian or China?' And I says, 'No Ma'am', I says, 'I'm just a bittie sunburnt after my holiday.' Well, you know, she laughed. She laughed and she says, Oh Moderator', she says, 'what a wag you are. Come away in about', she says, 'and meet some of the Privy Council. They're up for a meeting.' 'Oh yes, the Privy Council', I says, 'And what room do they meet in?' Well you know she laughed again. And after she had explained the joke to Willie Whitelaw, Willie laughed as well. In fact, he took a fit o' the splutters. I think a bit o' his jeely piece had gone down the wrong way. I thocht he was going tae dae himsel an injury. But no, no, in about to the rescue comes Norman Tebbit and gives him a right thump on the back – with his clenched fist . . .

Well, that was the Friday afternoon of course, but on the Friday evening, we had the Ghillies' Ball. Oh, what a rare night it was, the Ghillies' Ball. Ye've heard of the Glen Miller Sound? Well, we danced to the Jack Sinclair noise. Oh, he's a great chap Jack, though, for all that. He gave us one of these novelty prize dances. He said 'Now, ladies and gentlemen', he says, 'the first gentleman up to the platform carrying his partner's tights.' Well, I was dancing with Mrs Thatcher. And what a struggle we had. Eventually, I just had to say to her, 'Oh dinna bother, my dear. I'll take off my Moderator's gaiters'.

Well, that was the Ghillies' Ball. There was some drink consumed, I'll tell you. But next morning, my ecclesiastical hangover not withstanding, I was doon for my breakfast at the crack o' dawn. I had grapefruit, I had cornflakes, I had porridge and cream, and sausage and bacon and egg and tomato and fried bread and kidneys and black puddings. I had tea and toast and marmalade and rowies nae tae mention twa or three kippers and an Arbroath smokie. Well, after about an hour and a half o' this, I says to the Duke of Edinbugh, 'Do you know what we're getting for wir lunch? And the Duke says, 'Well, Moderator', he says, 'do you like salmon?' And I says 'Oh, I like a bit o' salmon fine enough, you know', and he says 'Well, it's just as well, Moderator', he says, "cos it's aye salmon in this place.' He says, 'It's that mither-in-law o' mine', he says, 'She's aye pleiterin' about wi' her fishin' rod catchin' the bloomin' things.' He says, 'You know Moderator', he says, 'we're just oot the door wi' salmon.'

Well, my dear friends, you know this, all the time that the Duke was spikkin', who should be standing in the doorway, but the Queen mother, her waders up tae her oxters, and huddin' up this big twenty-five pounder. 'Oh', says the Duke, 'Oh! What a beauty, Nana. I do hope we're getting that for wir dinner.' And you know, we did, we did get it for wir dinner, wi' a great aipple stuck in its mou'. Lovely dinner of course, wi' the full range of wines. But I just stuck tae the champagne. 'Cos I like a fizzy drink. After dinner too, of course, I should let you know that I was sitting next to Prince Andrew. What a very charming

young man Prince Andrew is. Prince Andrew says, 'Moderator', he says, 'I'd like to introduce you to my companion.' He says, 'This is Miss Katie Rabbit.' And I says, 'Oh yes, good evening Miss Rabbit, I'm very pleased to make your acquaintance you know.' And then I gives Prince Andrew a nudge and, 'Aye, aye', I says, 'Fit's it like switchin' fae a Koo tae a Rabbit?'

Well, after a very very cheery dinner, all the ladies withdrew leaving the lads to their port. And oh, what a rammy there wis. What a shindig there wis. Well, I'll tell you, that Nigel Lawson, he knows every word o' *The Ball o' Kirriemuir*. And things were just at their height, at about half past two in the morning, when who should appear in the doorway again, but the Queen Mother! She had come down in her dressing gown. Well, a hush fell on the company, and the Duke of Edinburgh went as white as a sheet. He's affa feart at his mither-in-law. And he says, 'Oh Moderator,' he says, 'we're in for a right rocket here.' But no, not a bit of it. In she comes, wi' a big joog o' cocoa and a great hillock o' salmon sandwiches.

Pair o' dookers Victorian bathing drawers recently considered by the Vestments Sub-Committee of the General Assembly as a possible replacement for the démodé gaiters.

Jeely piece Afternoon tea delicacy much loved by gluttonous English schoolboys (overgrown).

Jack Sinclair N.E. band-leader, disciple of Glen-fiddich rather than Glen Miller.

Rowie Auchterturra name for the Aberdeen buttery.

Pleiterin' Semi-immersion.

Pleiterin' a-boot Semi-immersion wearing waders.

Oxters Part of human anatomy susceptible to yokieness.

Katie Rabbit Bonny lassie, very nearly became Duchess of York.

Koo Bonny lassie, nae chance of ever bein' Duchess of York.

'ICE-CREAM'

nerve they've got; neen o' them can ever be A native Scot—a—— like me——

Ice-Cream

I can busk at the pia-ano,
Singing Nea-polita-ano,
'Cos I am Italia-ano
But second generation.
Si, my Da an' Ma –
They left Italy when I was twa,
Tae come-a here tae Bonnie Scotland.
They'd a clever scheme
Tae sell Italian ice-a-cream
In Scotland in a small café

So in 1922 they came
Ower tae Scotland for tae mak their hame.
Mony mair Italians did the same –
They spread a' ower Scotland.
Which is why to-day
Nearly ev'ry Scots community
Has got its ain-a ice-cream parlour,
And it's name's an un-
Mistakeably Italian one –
The ice-cream café
Mafi-
A!

175

But Italian ice-a-cream cafés
Are-a gravely threatened nowadays,
For there's other nationalities
Invading our patch-a.
Oh, the Indians come
With their curry and their poppadum.
The Chinese with-a chop-a suey;
There's-a folk fae France
Who have opened fancy restaurants,
An' ev'ry year mair chancers come.

From the States there come Kentucky fries
And McDonald's Fast Food Enterprise.
There are Arab places where sheep's eyes
Are served to you in aspic.
Me – I canna live
If it gets much mair competitive.
These foreigners all should be deported.
I'd kick oot that lot,
Fan ye think o't, fit a nerve they've got –
Neen o' them can ever be
A native Scot-a like me.

Welcome to the World's Bowlers

Beneath a banner proclaiming 'World Bowls Championships – Aberdeen 1984'
Councillor Alexander Swick is about to address a large gathering of bowlers from all
over the world.

Ladies and gentlemen, mesdames et messieurs (*he winks*), senores y senoras, herren und kippers. Ha, ha, ha! Jist a joke, jist a joke. Nae need tae get touchy aboot it, Heinrich. Bloomin' Germans. Nae sense o' humour, that's their trouble.

Now it is my privilege today to launch the kick-off o' this wonderful Championships, and to welcome the brotherhood of the world's bowlers to the breath-taking splendour of the Westburn Park. I am here today in place of the Lord Provost. He is deeply sorry he cannot be with you, but he has a prior engagement. He's had tae ging tae Fine Fare for his messages. Mind you, onything tae dae wi' sport, ye're better aff wi' me onywye. Was I not the Scottish Gas Board jogger of the year? Did I not win the Star and Garter sponsored walk all the way tae the Grill an' back? Was I not runner-up to Provost Collie in the St. Nicholas Hoose Japanese Sumo Wrestling championship?

This is nae the first time I've deen my stuff at the Westburn Park. In my young day there wis a lot o' good sports at the Westburn Park. But it is the first time I have performed in the middle of the bowling green before such a large audience.

Now my task today is a simple one. Or they widna hae gi'en me the job. It is tae say a few words of welcome tae try tae mak a' you foreigners feel at hame. Now, there are thirty-seven different nations represented here, but my message to you all today is this. We're a' Jock Tamson's bairns. I dinna ken fa Jock Tamson wis, but he must hiv had a very fast bike.

But we are all his bairns. We are all brothers under the skin. If I'm not mistaken, I see one or two black faces here today. You, sir. Where have you come here from? Ellis & McHardy. I see. You, sir, wi' the bush hat and the boomerang and the kangaroo on the lead. Far div you come fae? Perth. Wis the road busy comin' up this mornin'? It's an affa road that. A' that heavy lorries. It's a bloomin' scandal.

Fit aboot you Jim? Far div you come fae? Spain? I've been tae Spain. I've been twice tae Spain. Last year I wis on a package holiday tae Torremolinos. Three wiks for thirty-five quid. But much earlier, as a young man, I went off to the squalour and devastation of the Spanish Civil War. And I'll tell ye this. It wisna near as bad as Torremolinos. Ah yes, the Spanish Civil War. I wis very friendly wi' Guernica, you know.

Now fa else hiv we got? Gee whiz, some o' you boys is an affa ticket. Look at 'at boy there. Fit a wye tae ging aboot. You're an affa ticket, min. Ye're nae gan back tae yer digs like that, are ye? Far's yer digs? They winna let ye in. Nae wearin' a loin-cloth. No, nae even in the Malacca. An' the Bowling Green Committee's affa strict aboot dress. Ye canna wear that loin cloth on the bowling green. Dinna tak it aff, dinna tak it aff!

And what about you sir? Aye, you, wearin' the ceremonial head-dress and wi' the boar's tusk though your nose. Which team do you play for? England? In that case, sir, perhaps I should warn you that the local punters may, in fact will, mak you and the rest o' the English boys the target for some good-natured obscenities and light-hearted abuse. But I hope you will take it in the spirit in which it is intended: genuine and sincere hatred.

Right, fit's next? Oh aye. Now ye a' ken the arrangements for playin' on this green. It's 50p for half an 'oor, an' if yer match isna finished in half an 'oor, it's too bad, Ye're aff. Well, we've a lot o' matches tae get through. This is the World Championships 'is, ye ken. We canna scutter aboot. An' I'll tell ye anither thing. You, Buster, ye canna ging on til a bowlin' green wi' feet like 'at! Ye've got tae wear slips. Slips. Dinna be cheeky, madam. You, there. Boy George wi' the high-heeled boots. It's you I'm spikkin' til. I'm nae carin' if ye are the champion o' Colorado. Nae Colorado beetle-crushers on that grass. Look at it. Look at that grass. It's like a bowlin' green.

Now, boys, are ye happy enough wi' yer billets? 'Cos we've went tae a lot o' trouble tae get the richt digs for ye. You boys fae Holland. A'richt in the Dutch Mill? Far's the party fae Basutoland? Hands up. Hands up, Basutoland. Are you boys a' richt in the Treetops? An' fit aboot you Irish boys. You should be a' richt – we've pit you in the Station. fit d'ye mean? Naebody telt ye fit platform. In the name o'. . .

And now to my peroration. Having read the weather forecast for the next fortnicht, and realising that ye'll be gettin' some real Aiberdeen summer weather, may I end by saying, 'God bless these championships and all who sail in them.'

World Bowls Championships These were in fact held in the Westburn Park, Aberdeen in July, 1984.

Heinrich Retired bank manager, now President of Munchen Gladbach Bowling Club.

Ellis and McHardy Quondam purveyors of high quality shilbottle and Best English (see *Coal*).

Ticket Rough track (see *Wedding Guests*).

The Hot Line

Sandy Thomson is dialling a number on a modern digital telephone. In time to the dialling he is humming The Star Spangled Banner.

Sandy Thomson: Hello. Is that Washington, D.C.? is that you, Mr. President? Is it nae? Is that nae Washington? Fit? It's the exchange at Rhynie? Is that you, Beldie? But I've jist deen International Direct Diallin' richt through tae Washington. Fit wye did I nae get through? Fit? Ye've ta'en the plug oot o' the satellite? Tae bile the kettle for yer coffee. Well, wid ye hang up, an' wid you pit me through? Washington 4840. Thank you. Fit a vratch she is, that Beldie. She gets nae better.

Hello, hello. Is that you, Mr. President? Fit like, Ronnie? Howdy, old timer. Sandy Thomson here. No – fae Rhynie. No, you dinna ken me, but I've kent you a' my days. I mind gan tae see ye at the Huntly Playhoose. Wi' my Grannie. It wis *The Hasty Heart*. You wis a wounded sodger, an' ye wis affa good. Richard Todd wis affa good in that. Div ye ever hear fae Richard nowadays? No? Funny the wye ye lose touch wi' folk. It wis the same for me wi' a boy I kent in the Army. He wis a cockney. Fae Lambeth. Spoke funny kind. We wis great chums, but we didna keep up. Oh, there wis a Christmas card for five or six year. But I never sent *him* een, so he stopped. I thocht it wis real nesty o' him. Of course, he's maybe deid. It widna be sae bad if he wis deid.

Well, well, but I'll tell ye fit I'm phonin' aboot, Ronnie. Me an' some o' the boys wis haein' a drink last nicht in *The Glaikit Stirk*, an' we were jist takin' a'thing through hand, an' an affa argy-bargy got up. Now, you winna ken this, but Bert Cassie – d'ye ken Bert? No? – well, Bert gets affa heich fan he's spikkin' through drink. An' he got on tae the world situation, an' the nuclear arms race, an' Star Wars, an' medium an' lang range missiles, an' yer American policy, an' – fit? Ye're absolutely richt, Ronnie, I couldna pit it better mysel': fit a kirn the hale thing is. An' fit we want tae ask you, Ronnie, is this. Div ye ken fit ye're daein', min? Ye dinna. Ach, weel, I widna worry aboot it, no. I mean, Bert Cassie's on the Gordon District Cooncil, an' he says *they* dinna ken fit *they're* daein'. Mind you, if a district cooncil disna ken fit it's daein', it's nae the end o' the world. But if you dinna ken fit ye're daein', it's a bittie different, aye.

Hello. Here, jist a minutie, Ronnie. There's somebody else picked up anither phone somewye. There's somebody else on the line. *(He transfers the phone to his other ear)* Hello. Fa's that? Cher fa? Chernenko? Ye're spikkin' fae Moscow. Konstantin Chernenko. We're fairly in the big time today. Aye aye, Konnie, I'm sorry. Div – you – understand – fit – I – am – saying? Fit? You spik English. Answer the question. D'ye understand fit I'm sayin'? Ye div. An' ye're tryin' tae get through tae President Reagan on the hot line. Is it important? Are ye gan tae be on for long? 'Cos if ye are, ye'd be better waitin' till efter six o'clock an' get the cheap rate. Fit's 'at? Ye're in an affa hurry 'cos ye're rushin'. I ken ye're Russian.

Oh, rushin' awa'. Tae get yer paper. This is the nicht ye dae Fix the Ba' in *Pravda*. Fit's 'at? Oh, aye, I'll gie President Reagan a message for ye. Fit's the message? Fit ye sayin' til't? Fairly. Tie, tie. Michty me. Guid sakes. Losh be here. Nuclear war? Next Setterday? Ye canna hae a nuclear war next Setterday, it's the Oldmeldrum Sports! Well, well, but I'll fairly pass that message on tae Ronnie for ye. Cheeri-bye. Sorry, Auf Weidersensky. *(He transfers the phone back to his other ear).*

Hello. Are ye aye there, Ronnie? Now, listen, 'cos I've got a message for ye. It's a message fae Konnie. Ronnie. Fit d'ye mean, ye dinna ken ony Konnie, Ronnie? This is Konstantin Chernenko. Div ye nae ken fa Chernenko is? Ronnie, he's the top man in Russia. No, no, Ronnie. Stalin's deid. This is Chernenko. Well, maybe you dinna ken him. But he kens you. An' he disna like ye. He wis jist sayin', in *The Hasty Heart* he preferred Richard Todd.

Onywye, he's wantin' tae hae a meetin' wi' ye. A summit. No, no, Ronnie, nae a semmit. A Summit. Far aboot? Onywye ye like as lang's it's nae Washington. He winna ging tae Washington. An' you winna ging tae Moscow? 'Cos it's ower like Dundee. Weel, but there's nae problem. Meet half-wye. Come tae Rhynie! Oh, we'll pit on a good do for ye at Rhynie. Eh? Security? Nae problem, we'll get ye a secret hide-out at Clatt. Naebody will ever find ye at Clatt. Clatt. Hiv ye never heard o' Clatt? Well, there ye are. It's a secret, intit? Well, my brither, Willie, he bides at Clatt. He works at Rhynie but he bides at Clatt, an' maist nichts fan he gings hame, even *he* canna find Clatt.

Fit's 'at? Catering arrangements? Oh, we'll get the Station Hotel tae dae the caterin'. An' if onything can cement east-west relations, it's the Station Hotel stovies.

Vratch Rhynie call-girl.

Richard Todd Matinee idol very popular in the Cabrach.

A cockney fae Lambeth Quaint unsophisticated native of the orient.

The Glaikit Stirk Pub: Formerly the Stupid Stot; soon, following take-over, to be the Stakis Auchterturra Hydro.

Argy-bargy The stage in a public house exchange between a crack (or blether) and a stooshie. (see *Parents' Night*).

Affa heich fan he's spikkin' through drink. *In vino altissimus.*

Fit a kirn the hale thing is. Official State Department view of East-West relations.

Stalin Russian B-movie heavy, clearly a contemporary of President Reagan. Stalin began his career as an extra in *The Battleship Ptomenkin* and later, moving to America, had a successful career in Holywood where he worked under the name of Joan Crawford.

Semmit Thermal under garment confined these days to the North American incontinent.

Mounthooly   (AG)

(Tune: Manhattan)

Darling, though I love our fully
Furnished flat just off Mounthooly,
Money on rent
Isn't well spent.
Though we're cosy in our little
Hideaway behind the Spital,
We're in a groove,
Time now to move.

We'll leave Mounthooly,
And, sweetheart, you'll e –
Scape from care;
We'll buy a *pied a terre*
Somewhere.
One of these days Ah'll
Drive up to Hazal –
Head with you,
Where there are one or two
Nice houses with a stu –
Pendous view.
Or if I press, would
You fancy Desswood
Place maybe,
Or is the place for thee
Footdee?
To own somewhere would be grand;
We'll move, as we've always planned,
Out of Mounthooly
Into the promised land.

We'll take a chance in
A former manse in
Gladstone Place –
No heat or light but lots of space.
Or if we're shiftin',
Why not to Clifton
Road, my dear,
My cousin, Bessie Weir,
Bade there for twenty year –
'Course, she's queer.

What Aberdeen street
Compares with Skene Street?
Tell me, please.
Get to His Majesty's
With ease.
Together, dear, hand in hand
We'll fly to our love-nest, and
We'll be like Alice –
We'll be in Wonderland.

Princess Diana
Would like Devanha
Gardens West.
Mind you, it's hard to know where's best.
In all this jungle
A Stewartie's bungal –
Ow might suit,
With a disposal chute,
By means of which you put
Rubbish oot.
Bucksburn or Murcar,
Bieldside or Urquhart
Road let's try;
There's some place you and I
Could buy.
We'll borrow a hundred grand
And just like we always planned,
We will be living
In Never-Never Land.

Argyle Street

(Tune: Mounthooly)

Though we're lucky, dear, to rent a
Flat quite near the city centre,
Money on rent
Isn't well spent.
Though it's true we've been ecstatic
In our smart Argyle Street attic,
We're in a groove,
Time now to move.

But where in Glasgow
Can lad and lass go?
Don't despair.
We'll find a *pied a terre*
Somewhere.
We'll go to Yoker,
Where lots of folk are
Happy, dear;
My cousin, Bessie Weir,
Bade there for forty year –
'Course she's queer.
Or else for starters,
Let's try Cathcart or
Rutherglen
Just for a year, and then
Bearsden.
To own somewhere would be grand;
We'll move, as we've always planned,
Out of Argyle Street
Into the promise land.

People are full of
Praise for the School of
Art, my dear,
And there are flats, I hear,
Quite near.
Could there be any
Designed by Rennie
Mackintosh?
If we could buy one – Gosh!
Your Ma would say, 'Oh, losh,
'Zat no posh?'

Or you'd adore a
Hoose handy forra
Ubi Chip –
Whisky three quid a nip
Plus tip.
Together, dear, hand in hand
We'll fly to our love-nest, and
We'll be like Alice,
We'll be in Wonderland.

There's no disputin'
A house in Newton
Mearns would be
A stylish pad for thee
And me.
In all this jungle
A Barratt's bungal-
Ow might suit,
With a disposal chute,
By means of which you put
Rubbish oot.
Knightswood or Partick,
Where winds are Arctic
In July –
There's some place you and I
Could buy.
We'll borrow a hundred grand
And just like we've always planned,
We will be living
In Never Never Land.

Corstorphine

(Tune: Argyle Street or Mounthooly, according to taste)

Darling, though we're quite well off in
Our apartment near Corstorphine,
Money on rent
Isn't well spent.
Though we love our nice three-room house
In a cul-de-sac in Broomhouse,
We're in a groove,
Time now to move.

In South Queensferry
It can be very
Nice, you know,
Let's change our status quo
And go.
Or else, by golly,
We'll buy near Holy-
Rood my dear.
Mind you, the brew'ry's near;
It makes the atmosphere
Reek of beer.
Or Royal Circus
Or even Merchis-
Ton, I guess,
Would make a rather ness
Address.
To own somewhere would be grand;
We'll move, as we've always planned,
Out of Corstorphine
Into the promised land.

It thrilled us both, yon
Wee place in Lothian
Road last week.
It really was unique-
Ly chic.
Or hurry, hurry,
And buy near Murray-
Field, madame.
I hope to God I am
Still there to drink a dram
Next Grand Slam.
Like Jack and Jill in

Tranent or Gullane
We could be,
There's some place there for thee
And me.
Together, dear, hand in hand
We'll fly to our love-nest, and
We'll be like Alice,
We'll be in Wonderland.

Let's drive out through town,
Explore the New Town –
You'd like it.
We'd stay there for a bit,
Then flit.
In all this jungle
A Barratt's bungal-
Ow might suit,
With a disposal chute,
By means of which you put
Rubbish oot.
A Christopher Wren House,
Perhaps in Stenhouse
Or Dalry –
There's some place you and I
Could buy
We'll borrow a hundred grand
And just like we always planned,
We will be living
In Never Never Land.

Buying a House

A prospective purchaser, newspaper in hand, approaches the front door of a house which is for sale in a residential part of Aberdeen. He rings the door bell. The owner opens the door.

P.   *(Referring to the newspaper)* Is this 53 Walpole Avenue?

O.   Yes.

P.   A superior, modern, Georgian style, executive bungalow?

O.   Yes.

P.   Attractively situated in a highly prestigious West End location but convenient for the Fine Fare bus?

O.   Yes.

P.   For further particulars apply to Gorrod, Davie, Kemp and Walker. Well, that's a crowd o' sharks.

O.   Would you like to come in and see the house?

P.   Well, I'm nae here tae sell ye brushes.

O.   Come away in then. *(He ushers the purchaser in)* Now this is the hall.

P.   It may be a hall tae you. It looks like a lobby tae me.

O.   Well, it's just a hall. There's not much you can say about it.

P.   There's naething you can say about it. Except that it's a lobby. Fit's that thing on the wa' there?

O.   That's a genuine Polynesian hat stand.

P.   Is it a fixture?

O.   No.

P.   Thank God for that onywye.

   (They move into the first main room)

O. Now this is the lounge. This is the first public room.

P. I'll say it's public. The folk ootside can see richt intil't. Look, there's a wifie across the road starin' in. *(He waves)* Hello!

O. Now, the windows are fully double-glazed.

P. Oh? Is that for noise or heat?

O. Well, both.

P. You mean it lets in the noise and keeps oot the heat?

O. From the window you get a good view of the garden. Of course it's past it now.

P. Well, you should know, if anybody should. Here, far's the garage?

O. Well, there's no garage, but there's space for one.

P. Well, that'll fairly keep yer car dry. Tell me, are you leaving the pelmets?

O. If the purchaser wants them. They're no use to me where I'm going.

P. Oh! and what kind o' hippie kibbutz are you gan til that disna hae pelmets?

O. And the carpet can be taken over at valuation.

P. Valuation! I widna hae it in a gift.

O. Shall we go on? *(They go to the next room)* Here we go into the dining room. Sorry the table hasn't been cleared. But you know what it's like.

P. It's like a battle field, that's what it's like. And somebody hisna finished their potted heid. Gad sakes! *(He kicks open the door)* I will admit this is a fair-sized cupboard.

O. We usually call that the kitchen. It's a Poggenpohl kitchen. These are German units.

P. I'll say they're German units. They're like the 14th Panzers. And I suppose that makes you Field Marshal Rommel.

O. And that's the door to the back. Mind my bucket, would you.

P. Oh, I beg you bucket's pardon. God, that's an affa steep stair for the coal to come up an' the rubbish tae ging doon.

O. Shall we go down?

P. Nae unless we're roped thegither. Fa d'ye think I am? Sherpa Tensing?

O. Well, anyway, from here you can see the patio.

P. Patio? Twa or three slabs o' cement an' a nesty lookin' gnome. Is he a relative?

O. And that lawn runs right down to the back wall.

P. Lawn? What lawn? I've never seen a lawn wi' a whirligig on it. That's just a drying green. And it's a bit near the back lane, isn't it? The last hoose we were in my missus got her bloomers pinched aff the line. Are you bothered wi' back lane fetishists?

O. Fetishists? I'm a Loretto man myself. Now I'm sure you would like to see the bedrooms. Shall we go upstairs?

P. Lead on, Macbeth. *(they go upstairs. As they do so, the purchaser trips)* My God, that carpet's a death trap. And where are that ducks on the wall flying to? If you ask me, they're migratin'. Tae some place that's nae sae caul'.

(They enter the first room upstairs)

O. Now, this is the master bedroom. It has a luxury shower unit en suite.

P. Shower unit en suite? It's just a roosty cabinet – stickin' oot o' the press. Did you get plannin' permission for that? A boy I ken did something like that withoot plannin' permission and the hale hoose had tae come doon, once his brither-in-law had clyped on him – tae the K.G.B. in St. Nicholas Hoose

(They move on)

O. This is another bedroom. This has a vanity unit.

P. Ye mean a sink. Oh, we're washing wir smalls, are we? I use the expression loosely. Is that a cupboard?

O. Yes, everything gets thrown in there. You know what it's like when you've got a family.

P. Well, you may throw *your* family into a cupboard –

(They leave the second bedroom and enter the third one. They have to stoop to do so, and they stand inside it, knees bent, still stooping)

O. And this is the smallest bedroom.

P. This might just be alright for Simon.

O. Simon? Is that your son?

P. Wir son? It's wir Scottie. I wouldna put a human being in a hole like this.

(They back out carefully)

O. There's just one more room to see. And that's the bathroom. Shall I go first this time? *(He enters the bathroom)*

P. Here, is this floor level?

O. Well, it is at this side of the room and it is at the other side of the room, but there's a slight slope in the middle.

P. A slight slope? It's like the Tyrebagger! Fit's that patch up there?

O. Well, we've had a little trouble with dry rot.

P. Dry rot? It' soakin' weet!

O. As you can see, the whole bathroom – the suite, the tiling and the carpet – are all done in matching avocado green.

P. Aye, it's jist a pity aboot yer pink toilet roll. It's nae very conveniently situated. On the ither side o' the bath.

O. Well, I think you've seen the whole house now. Oh, as you can see, the ceiling is very well plastered.

P. Aye. Like the homer you got tae dae it.

O. Not at all. I did it myself.

P. Oh? What's your job?

O. I'm with the District Council.

P. The District Cooncil! Good afternoon.

O. What's wrong?

P. We ken the kind o' tricks the District Cooncil get up til.

O. What do you mean?

P. You're the lot that sells folk hooses that dinna belong tae ye!

Gorrod, Davie, Kemp and Walker Firm of seed merchants in Aberdeen, now apparently diversifying into estate agency.

Tyrebagger Steep hill on the A96 Aberdeen-Inverurie road; bowdlerisation of 'Tyre-bugger', so-called because of the effect it has on your re-moulds.

Field Marshal ('Sandy') Rommel Teutonic kitchen designer.

Sell hooses that dinna belong tae ye The District Council had recently done just that. Well it could happen to anybody.

Building Societies

Tune: *The Wee Cooper o' Fife.*

O, Union Street is beyond compare,
But something the visiting exile sees
Is the number of Building Societies there:
The Cheltenham & Gloucester, the whole merry roster
Of English Building Societies.

In Union Street soon there'll be no shops at all,
No rest'rants or cafés doing afternoon teas,
Just Buildings Societies wall to wall:
The Leeds and the Leicester and all of the rest of
Those English Building Societies.

Ordinary businesses cannot afford
To purchase a Union Street property.
But raising a mortgage is easy for –
The Woolwich, the Yorkshire,
The Cheltenham & Gloucester,
The Leeds and the Leicester
The Bristol & West – er –
The new Abbey National – trendy and fash'nable,
The Halifax, Anglia
And the Britannia,
(A)lliance and Gateway,
The Bradford and Bingley –
Those English Building Societies,

'THE RENTOKIL MAN'

The Rentokil Man

Throughout the city every day my merry trade I ply,
And no-one ever worries if I go driving by,
But if I stop, their eyes go pop –
I am a bogey man.
What kind of trade makes folk afraid?
I drive a Rentokil van.
       And people take fright
       If next door they catch sight
       Of a station'ry Rentokil van.

To rich man's row, to poor man's lane, to households great and small,
Dry rot makes no distinction: in time it comes to all.
Then from behind Venetian blind
The neighbours, if they can,
Will have a teet along the street
To watch the Rentokil van.
  The drop would appal you
  In property value
  That comes with a Rentokil van.

For if you should observe my van outside your neighbour's door,
It means they must have got dry rot in roof and walls and floor,
And if they've got the dread dry rot,
What surer prospect than
That it creeps through, and soon you too
Will need the Rentokil van.
  And the bill's in four figures,
  (And sometimes must bigger)
  That follows a Rentokil van.

But if my van speeds past your street, it makes you cock-a-hoop,
It's nice to think that somewhere someone else is in the soup.
You can't avoid the *schadenfreude* –
Suppress it, if you can –
When some poor bum, perhaps a chum,
Requires a Rentokil van.
  Life somehow seems brighter,
  If some other blighter
  Requires a Rentokil van.

But while my van attacks dry rot in other parts of town,
That fatal fungus strikes my house, which now is falling down,
I'm told that I can't occupy
My house for longer than
At most, two days – oh! what disgrace –
For me, a Rentokil man.
  The whole thing's bewild'rin'
  For my wife and children
  When Dad is a Rentokil man.
  Though fam'lies ought not to,
  Tomorrow we've got to
  Move into the Rentokil van.

Teet A swift act of unobserved surveillance. First used as a surreptitous glance at page 3 of a foostie newspaper (q.v. – *Under the Carpet*)

The Bridegroom

A bridegroom, Export can in hand, addresses the wedding guests.

Reverend Morrison, ladies and gentlemen. On behalf of myself and my – wife .
. . gie's a chance boys, gie's a chance! Oh no, fair play fair play! . . . On behalf of
Lorraine and myself, there's just twa or three folk I want tae say thanks very
much til, ken?

An' the first een's wir best man, that's just proposed the toast tae Lorraine and
me's health. So, thanks very much Bill, for keeping it clean. Well, pretty clean.
Well a lot cleaner than we thocht it was gan tae be. Mind you, even so, Bill, I
thocht yer last joke was a bitty . . . ken . . . so-so . . . ken fit I mean . . . pretty dicey,
ken. Oh, I ken there was twa or three wyes ye could take it, but they were a' dirty,
Bill, . . . Eh? I'm nae caring if it was Lorraine that telt ye it.

Now, secondly, it's a big thank you to the minister, the Reverend Morrison . . .
Fit's that Mr. Morrison? . . . Henderson! . . . Come again? . . . Paterson! Weel, fit
ever yer name is, I thocht ye did a magic job wi' the service. I thocht it was ace!
Ye ken? A' that singin' an' prayin' . . . Magic! I couldna fault ye on it, Mr.
Donaldson. And Lorraine thocht it was lovely an' a'. Didn't ye, Lorraine?
Lorraine, use yer hunky darling! Sorry, sorry, Mr. Ferguson, but Lorraine an'
me, we've never been in a kirk afore, and it was affa good o' ye tae keep us richt
on a' the details, ken? a' the procedures. Ken fit I mean? I mean, until you telt
me, I had nae idea I was supposed tae gie the minister a thirty quid book token.
So, thanks very much . . . Mr Williamson.

Now, fa's next? Oh aye, for wir lovely new hoose, we're very, very grateful tae
Lorraine's brother Ronnie, that works in the housing department. I understand we are the youngest couple ever tae be allocated sheltered housing. So,
thanks very much, Ronnie. And I'm sure it winna be lang afore ye get another
job.

And then of course, a very big thank you to Lorraine's mum and dad, Mr. and
Mrs. Dawson, for laying on this lovely big reception, here the day, in the Conservative Club. Noo, kennin' foo skint Mr. Dawson usually is, I'll bet ye got a
shock, did ye? fan ye saw the size o' this reception that he's laid on here the day.
But I ken there's a lot o' lead, aff a helluva lot o' roofs, has went intae this reception, and I ken the size o' the bill that's waitin' for Mr. Dawson, when he comes
oot o' Peterheid Prison.

Now in the unavoidable absence of Mr. Dawson, detained during her Majesty's pleasure – though fit pleasure she gets oot o' Bert Dawson bein' in the jile I
dinna ken – we wis stuck, wis we, for somebody tae gie awa' the bride, and we're
very, very grateful tae Lorraine's Uncle Alex, for coming straight fae his work in

the slaughterhoose. And if ye dinna ken Alex, that's him ower there wi' the carnation in his dungarees. Stan' up an tak a bow Alex! ... Oh, he canna get up, the bleed's congealed on his dungarees.

And then, it's thanks very much tae my ain uncle Bob for makin' a video o' the wedding. Nice one Bob! Mind you, I still think it would have been better if you'd ta'en us tae the Winter Gardens in the Duthie Park like a'body else. Better than yer plot at Airyhall. I mean, I ken Lorraine was affa keen tae get a backgroond o' flooers – but nae cauliflooers.

Now, finally, afore I sit doon, this has got tae be the day, is it? that I mak my peace wi' Mrs. Dawson, Lorraine's mum. I mean, it's nae secret, is it Mrs. Dawson, that you an' me, we hinna exactly seen eye tae eye, ken fit I mean? I think it a' began the very first night I took Lorraine hame. It wisna sae much the wye ye looked at me, Mrs, Dawson, it was the wye ye said 'Get the hell oot the bloody hoose an' never come back!' But I could tak a hint. And I never did ging back. Nae fan you were there, onwye. Well, well, but that's a' in the past, is it, Mrs. Dawson? I mean efter a lovely wedding like this the day, I think we're a' gan tae get on fine. Ken fit I mean? 'Cos I can mind fan my sister got mairred, on the day o' the weddin', my mither had a wee greet. And I said tae her, 'Fit ye greetin' for Ma?' and she said 'I'm greetin' 'cos I'm happy.' Well, Mrs Dawson, you must be ecstatic!' 'Cos you hinna stopped greetin' a' day! In fact, for the sake o' the guests, would ye brighten up. I mean, ye was greetin' a' the wye through that lovely service that we got fae the Reverend Robertson. And now ye've been greetin' a' the wye through this weddin' breakfast. Funny, is it, haein' yer breakfast in the efterneen. But we had tae hae it in the efterneen, so's Lorraine wouldna be bothered wi' her mornin' sickness.

Musical Family

Beethoven – Choral Symphony

If I calmly view my family
I cannot avoid the thought
What a very 'str'ordinary
Bunch of relatives I have got.
Father, mother, sister, brother,
Daft on music if you please;
All my cousins – several dozens–
Smitten by the same disease.

Strauss – Fledermaus Overture

I've an Uncle Sandy,
He is bald and bandy
And he's got nac teeth,
But in spite of this deficiency
He can whistle maist efficiently.
He's the orra man at
Mains of Tilliescannet
Seven miles fae Keith;
As he plighters in the sharn there,
He is whissallin' like stink.

He's in an ecstatic state often,
Whistlin' Debussy or Beethoven.
If a bull has a hoast or a horse a cough,
He soothes it with Rimsky Korsakov.

Mendelssohn – Violin Concerto

My mither's
Big brither's
A lump
Upon his rump
The doctor took one good look
And then diagnosed a plook.

My uncle's
Carbuncle –
At first it wisna sair
Now he's critically ill
In Foresterhill
He's baffled them up there.
Said a nurse wi' a smile
'That's the very first bile
To require intensive care'

Handel – Water Music

I've one mair Auntie – my Auntie Bunty,
She bides in the country – twa miles oot o' Huntly
She's jist got mairried again –
A master plumber ca'd Len.
She'd had nine previous men,
And then came Len.
He's Auntie Bunty's Number Ten.
Len's plumber's business
Is at its briskest
Jist efter Christmas.
Folk lose their reason
When they are bleezin'
An' pipes are freezin'.
A pipe burst on Hogmanay,
Folk dinna care fit they pay,
'Cos it's a helluva mess
Haein' water a' ower the place.
Frantic they dash for the 'phone,
Then comes the call,
And they'll pay old Lennie any price at all.
They're skint – and he maks a mint.
Just mention water to Len and he will smile;
From water plumbers make their pile.
And that is why all the time a plumber plumbs,
The Water Music's what he hums.

Ravel – Bolero

There's quite a few fat wifies in Aiberdeen,
But I think my Auntie Jean
Must be the fattest that I've seen,
So it's a shock to find she's very keen
On Ravel's Bolero.

She first heard it watchin' the T.V.,
Watchin' the skatin' – well, big, muckle Jean
Indentifies wi' Torvill an' Dean,
She worships their Bolero routine.
And the tune – well, as she said tae Bertha, her freen',
'Hear that tune? Fit a beaut.
It knocks me oot.'

Jean, never mindin' foo much money she spent,
To the record shop she went,
To buy that disc was her intent.
Now it's fantastic, she's completely sent
By Ravel's Bolero.

She gings dancin' roon' about the hoose
To the Bolero, though the tune disna suit
The muscles and the bones of big Jean,
The twenty-seven stones of big Jean.
What is more, sung in the dulcet tones of big Jean
The Bolero is hell –
Even for Ravel.

If a bull has a hoast If a bull is visited by a respiratory infection.

Torvill and Dean Auchter Torvill and Aber Dean, famous N.E. ice-skating partnership.

The Burns Supper

Buff: Earlier this year we were guests at a Burns Supper given by Aberdeen District Council at which the address to the haggis was delivered by a man, Scottish to the core, Caledonian through and through, the Chairman of the Scottish Tourist Board.

(Enter the Tourist Chief, wearing Chieftain's cocket bonnet. He speaks in the plummy strangulated tones of the Sloane rather than the Glasgow Ranger.)

Fair fa yah
Honest sonsie face,
Great chieftain o'
The pudden race.
Weel are ye worthy o' a grace
As lang's my airm.

There can be few Scots who do not thrill to hear the poetry of our national bard *(he pauses to consult a note which he has in his hand)* Robert Burns, expressed as it is so vigorously in the dialect we hold so dear. Lang live our auld Scots tongue.

For it is a proud thing to be a Scot. Hail Caledonia, stern and wild, heedorum hoderum, foo's yer neeps and tak' the High Road up the leg o' yer kilt. These stirring words, spoken by Burns' great contemporary, Sir Walter Scott, on the eve of his historic journey to the South Pole, are a constant reminder that we Scots have much to be proud of. And not just wee Scots, but big Scots too.

But what sort of a Scot was Robert Burns? Well, of course, he would have been very much at home in the Scottish Conservative Party today: he lived in the eighteenth century. He was a robust, earthy man, a son of the soil, very much loved by the people of Ayr-shah. It wasn't that for the people of Ayr-shah he was a father figure; for at least half the county he actually was their father.

Robert Burns was very fond of Scotland's national dish, known at that time as Bonnie Mary of Argyll – no relation to the present Duchess.

But to return to the haggis, it seems to me that Scotland is very like a haggis. Scotland, you see, has got plenty of guts. Like the haggis, Scotland's outward appearance is grey and sodden, and its constituents are simple and coarse, and with a proven propensity for turning the Prime Minister's stomach – a propensity which is warmly reciprocated.

So, it gives me great pleasure to propose the toast to the haggis, coupled with the name of our hosts this evening, Aberdeen District Council. The toast is 'The Haggis and the Neeps.'

We've No Business

Tune: There's No Business Like Show Business.

The mis'rable matinees in Airdrie or Troon,
Far naebody can understand us richt;
The Mondays in Methil, the Sundays in Scone,
The Chinese meals at twelve o'clock at nicht;
The bloomin' nuisance pittin' on makeup –
That's when my dermatitis plays me up.

We've no business in Show Business,
We're too long in the tooth.
Show biz folk are young and sharp and trendy,
We're jist squares – we're no hypoten-use.
It's nae much fun to be the geriatric
In a theatric-
Al boarding hoose.

There's no people like show people,
Or so people maintain.
But we have not met Gielgud or Olivier,
Frank Sinatra's not come our way,
Elton John once passed us on the Motorway,
But he didna see us –
We were in a bus.

At Christmas we don't get a gift or a card
From Terry Wogan or from Jimmy Young.
The old Beechgrove Gard'ners, now, they're nae sae hard,
George Barron eence gied me a load o' dung.
We've not got into drugs – we tak' instead
Twa Rennies on wir wye up tae wir bed.

We've no business in Show Business,
It's no business for us.
There's nae excitement daein' a show in Thurso:
Nae magic in a Lerwick Hogmanay,
Nae glamour in a Nissen Hut in Girvan,
Whatever Irvin'
Berlin may say.

We've no business in Show Business,
'Cos business can be thin.
You try to count the audience in the overture:
There's sixty folk there – it's pretty poor,
And most of them are Cockneys on a Saga tour.
We wish we could be gone –
But –
The show's got to go on.
That's show Business!

ROYAL LYCEUM THEATRE
FESTIVAL DIARY

London Festival Ballet's
LFB2
New Works
11–13 August at 7.30 pm   Matinée 13 August at 2.30 pm

Market Theatre of Johannesburg
BORN IN THE RSA
14–16 August at 7.30 pm   Matinée 16 August at 2.30 pm

Nuria Espert Company
YERMA
By Lorca
18–20 August at 7.30 pm   Matinée 20 August at 2.30 pm

Compania de Jose Luis Gomez
BLOOD WEDDING
By Lorca   SUPPORTED BY THE INSTITUTE OF SPAIN
22–24 August at 7.30 pm   Matinée 23 August at 2.30 pm

SCOTLAND THE WHAT
22, 23 August at 11.00 pm   28–30 August at 10.45 pm

Théâtre de la Salamandre
LE SAPERLEAU
By Gildas Bourdet   WITH ASSISTANCE FROM THE ASSOCIATION
26, 27 August at 7.30 pm   FRANÇAISE D'ACTION ARTISTIQUE

Market Theatre of Johannesburg
ASINAMALI
28–30 August at 7.30 pm   Matinée 30 August at 2.30 pm

Tickets available from the Festival Box Office 21 Market Street
Credit cards 225 5756.

Song of the Scottish M.P's

Tune: *The Deil's Awa' Wi' the Exciseman*

To sit in the Palace of Westminster
Is open to everybody,
And Scotland's Members of Parliament
Make a fascinating study.
Donald Dewar looks saft
Denis Canavan's daft
And what's obvious mair and mair is –
Dalyell's awa', Dalyell's awa',
Dalyell's awa' wi' the fairies.

The beer that bears George Younger's name
Is one of Scotland's features.
Malcolm Rifkind, though, is a whisky man,
Though he disna care for Teachers.
Robin Cook looks weird
Wi' his funny red beard,
Michael Ancram breeds canaries,
Bert McQuarrie plays darts,
Ron Brown supports Hearts,
And Dalyell's awa' wi' the fairies.

Woy Jenkins has a weakness –
It's for Burgundy and Stilton.
Gordon Wilson leads the Scottish Nats.,
Though he never has a kilt on.
Charles Kennedy looks
As though he reads books
About cowboys ridin' the prairies.
Willie Hamilton's keen
Tae get rid o' the Queen,
And Dalyell's awa' wi' the fairies.

David Steel would like to be P.M. –
His party's first since Lloyd George.
Nicky Fairbairn's wedding outfit made
Him look a bit like Boy George.
Norman Buchan aye sings
In a voice just like Bing's,
'Yestreen the Queen had four Maries.'
Donald Stewart is odd –
He won't drink at the Mod,
And Dalyell's awa' wi' the fairies.

The Belgrano Affair –
Well, he had something there,
And if Tam's a bit mad,
A' the rest are as bad.
Not just two or three –
Every Scottish M.P.
Each one of that breed,
They're a' wrang in the heid –
They're a' awa' wi' the fairies.

The Auchterturra Builder

A builder is discovered in an old dilapidated cottage, measuring-tape in hand, sizing up the interior. He is joined by a professor who is red in the face and out of breath.

P.   Sorry I'm late, Mr. Webster.

W.   Oh, but that's a' richt, Professor. I was lookin' oot the windae and I could see ye comin'.

P.   You had no trouble finding the place?

W.   Oh no, nane at a'. Yer directions was spot on. Five mile fae Rhynie. Five and a half fae Kennethmont. By Jove, ye're verra central here.

P.   Marvellous view!

W.   Grand view! Grand view! Was it the view ye bocht this place for now?

P.   No, not entirely. My wife and I always liked the idea of buying an old croft and doing a sympathetic conversion.

W.   Ah weel, ye've come tae the richt man. The last job I did was a conversion. Ye ken the Liesure Complex near Huntly? Squash coort, jacuzzi an' sauna? Three month ago it was a slatterhoose. Now ye canna get much mair sympathetic than that, can ye? Well, it's affa fine meetin' ye, Pro-

fessor, ken? Pittin' a face tae the voice on the telephone. An' fit is't you're a professor o', Professor?

P.   Well, I'm retired now, but I was professor of Rural Sociology.

W.   God almichty! Fit's that, now?

P.   Rural Sociology? Well, it's the application of scientific principles to the study of community structures and work patterns in a non-urban environment.

W.   Ye mean, fit it's like bidin' in the country?

P.   That's about it, yes.

W.   Aye. Have I just seen a bit aboot you in the paper? Ye've just written a great lang book aboot Aiberdeenshire? Eight hunner pages an' nivver a picter!

P.   Yes, actually it's a statistical socio-economic study. For example, it demonstrates that in the course of a year the average Aberdeenshire housewife makes five and a half trips into Aberdeen.

W.   Ye mean on the last trip she gets stuck in the Glens o' Foudlan'? Tell me Professor, fit did ye dae afore ye wis a professor, Professor?

P.   Oh, I've always been in the academic life.

W.   Oh, so ye've never worked? Never worked, and now ye've retired? 'At's good 'at, isn't it? Some boys have a' the luck!

P.   Actually I took early retirement under the University's voluntary severance arrangements.

W.   Oh, ye mean ye've been kicked oot?

P.   Oh, I've got my pension and my lump sum and we've just sold a big house in Aberdeen, so we're fairly well off.

W.   Oh! And yer wantin' a price fae me, for puttin' this place in order. Is that richt, Professor?

P.   Well, I'd like to get a few quotations. What other builders are there around here?

W.   Ye ken this, Professor? My mind has just gone a complete blank.

P. Isn't there someone in Alford?

W. Oh, I believe there is; a young loon just started up. Made a lovely job though, o' the dominie's new lock-up. It's jist a peety the car winna ging in.

P. Is there nobody else?

W. Oh now, there's a boy ower at Insch.

P. And has he just started?

W. No, he's just aboot finished. For the third time!

P. So, it looks as though I'm stuck with you!

W. Stuck wi' me? Stuck wi' this place is mair like it.

P. Oh, not necessarily, I can easily sell it again.

W. Sell this place? Fit kind o' feel gype would buy a place like this? It's just a rickle o' stanes. There's been naebody near this place for the last thirty year.

P. Well, the estate agent never told us that when he showed us round.

W. Fan did ye come oot tae see it?

P. Last month – end of June.

W. Oh, so ye hinna been here in December? Oh no, naebody's ever been here in December. It's usually March afore ye get in aboot tae this place. In fact it wis May last year.

P. I thought you said it hadn't been occupied for thirty years?

W. Well, it's been partially occupied.

P. Partially occupied?

W. Partially sheep and partially cattle. They used tae come in here in the bad weather. The really bad weather. It had tae be affa bad afore they'd come in here. 'Cos they're nae feel. Noo, tell me Professor, is this a Cooncil grant job?

P. Well, I don't know, I mean, I haven't had any plans done.

W. Ah, but we'll fairly get a plan for ye! We'll put in the plan o' the slatterhoose.

P. The slaughterhouse?

W. Aye, the plan o' that slatterhoose has never let me doon yet!

P. And do you think we'll get a grant?

W. Aye, a subsidie. Mind you, lookin' at yer gable end there, I some how think you've got a subsidie a'ready! Noo, we'll need to strauchen that oot!

P. I'm sorry?

W. Strauchen oot yer gable end. That'll be nine hunner pound. And that'll affect yer ties.

P. Ties?

W. Twelve hunner pound. And that'll affect yer timmers.

P. Timmers?

W. Fifteen hunner pound. An' ootside there's extra stane for yer wa's.

P. Wa's?

W. Nineteen hunner. Slates for yer reef, twa thoosand. Then of course, the hale place'll need pintin'.

P. Pintin'?

W. Aye, pintin'. Pintin' an' pentin'.

P. Pintin' an' pentin'?

W. And, pentin' an' pintin'. Now, that'll be twa thoosand four hunner, twa thoosand seven hunner, four thoosand five hunner, six thoosand seven hunner . . . Ca' it seven thoosand.

P. *Seven* thousand! Are you sure?

W. No, you're richt Professor, eight thoosand. Eight thoosand pound.

P. Now, the windows.

W. Well reminded, Professor. Fower windaes, a' needin' replacin'. A thoosand.

P. But we were thinking of double glazing.

W. Twa thoosand. Each. Twa thoosand, twa thoosand, twa thoosand, twa thoosand.

P. Do you realise that this place is recently listed?

W. Recently listed? It's aye listed! It's coupin' 'at wye. Ye've got a subsidie in the east. And ye're coupin' in the west. Now the next big question, Professor, is this. Div ye want a sneck on yer wattery door?

P. I'm sorry?

W. A sneck!

P. A sneck?

W. On yer wattery. A snib – for yer bathroom?

P. Oh, a snib!

W. Ye've got a bathroom, haven't ye?

P. Yes, the bathroom's through there.

W. Oh, that's far that bath got til! The last time I saw that bath it wis in the corner o' Jimmy Davidson's park. Wi' a slorach o' nowt roond aboot it.

P. A slorach o' nowt?

W. A puckly kye.

P. A puckly kye?

W. Twa or three coos.

P. Oh.

W. Now – div ye want a sneck on yer wattery?

P. Oh yes, yes.

W. Aye, ye're better wi' a sneck. Tae keep the nowt out.

P. To keep the nowt out?

W. Aye, because a beast'll aye come back tae its ain smell. Sneck on wattery, one hunner pounds.

P. A hundred pounds for a sneck?

W. Oh, but it'll be a big sneck! Now Professor, that's a' the bad news. Here is the good news! You winna need to spend a penny on rewiring.

P. Oh, good!

W. Because there's nae electricity. Electricity, ten thoosand pounds.

P. You know, it really looks as if we're going to have to economise in some areas. It's a great pity, 'cos my wife had set her heart on a luxury kitchen.

W. Fair enough, we'll leave the widden mangle. Leaving mangle, two hunner pounds.

P. But we don't want a mangle!

W. Removing mangle, four hunner pounds. Now we'll just tot this little lottie up for ye, an' see if we can get an accurate guesstimate, Professor.

P. Well, break it gently. I mean, my lump sum's only sixty thousand pounds.

W. Sixty thoosand! Oh, I can see that goin'.

P. You can see that going?

W. Just as clearly as I could see you comin'.

Rickle o' steens Best known characteristic of Doric architecture.

Ties, timmers, wa's, pintin' an' pentin' Luxury embellishments occurring only occasionally in Doric architecture.

Sneck on yer wattery The ultimate luxury in Doric architecture.

Slorach Defined in the *Concise Scots Dictionary* as 'a wet disgusting mess', as of cattle round a trough, in which circumstances a sneck on the watery is advised.

Cattle English for nowt, kye, beasts, stots, stirks, coos.

Snooker

Tune: Bonnie Mary of Argyll

I have watched Steve Davis sinking
Ten black balls and ten red;
As I watch him, I am thinking –
I must be off my head.
Great potting – no suggestion
Of human fault or fluff,
But I can't avoid the question:
Why do I watch this stuff? – and see the time,

It's 2 a.m. precisely,
And I should be in bed,
But Cliff Thorburn's snookered nicely –
Cue ball behind a red.
Of all my many follies
This addiction is the pick:
Watching grown men knock wee ballies
Round a table with a stick – at dead of night.

I sometimes wonder if it's
What life should be about,
Sitting watching Terry Griffiths
As the precious sands run out.
Did school or parents fail, or
Am I just a stupid twit,
To be hooked on Dennis Taylor
When I should be in my pit? I'm not alone –

From Sutherland to Surrey,
Like sheep, the nation flocks,
All hypnotised by Hurri-
Cane Higgins on the box.
I've a wife with whom I've found joy,
But now we never talk;
Instead I watch Doug Mountjoy

As he gives his cue a chalk – it's crazy!
Oh, it's nae for watchin' snooker
That man was given a brain;
I'm sure that's richt,
And so I'll watch the nicht
Something that's on a higher plane.

At this point there is heard over the P.A. the thud of a dart entering a dart board followed by the excited voice of a darts commentator proclaiming, 'One hundred and eighty!'

The Auchterturra By-Election

Newsnight

We hear the Newsnight *signature music and see a bespectacled character wearing glasses and clutching a microphone. He speaks and identifies himself as John Cole.*

J.C. John Cole here for *Newsnight* – and tonight, *Newsnight* brings you a Parliamentary By-Election Special from Auchterturra, Aberdeenshire. Auchterturra is a remote scattered constituency; in fact, its constituents aren't just scattered, they're usually plootered, and none more so than the Returning Officer, Councillor Alexander Swick, now retired, but formerly a town councillor in Aberdeen, where for many years he served on the committee for art galleries, museums and sewage works, to which he made a huge contribution. Later, he became Provost of Turriff, after leading the bloodless revolution known as 'The Turra Coup'. And now, here is the Returning Officer with the declaration.

Enter Alexander Swick, the Returning Officer, wearing a red gown and carrying the declaration document. He taps the microphone and blows into it.

A.S. Is this thing workin'? Hiv ye nae got it workin' yet, boys? Oh, gee! B.B.C.? Big Bloomin' Cock-up! Testing, 1-2-3- Mary had a little lamb, she also had a bear. I often saw her little lamb but I never saw her – testing, 1-2-3- O.K.? Can ye a' hear me. Right, this is the result the whole nation has been waiting for. Who will be the winner? And the winner is – *(He opens up the declaration document like the presenter at a T.V. awards ceremony)* Meryl Streep for *Take the High Road.* Ha! ha! Jist a joke, jist a joke. Eh? Weel, I'm only a District Cooncillor. It's nae as if I wis a *professional* comedian. Now, eyes down for the declaration. 'Parliamentary By-Election: Constituency of Auchterturra and Clatt. I, the under-signed –' Well, I hinna signed it yet, but I'm gan til. ' – being the Returning Officer, do hereby declare that the votes cast for each candidate was as follows:–
Davenport-Smythe, Sir Reginald.'

(A voice is heard over the P.A.)

P.A. Labour.

(The returning Officer looks around, mystified)

A.S. 5,512. Well done, Reggie. Pretty good for the only Militant in the Rotary. Farquharson, Thomas –

P.A. That's Tam the Poacher, Conservative Private Enterprise.

A.S. 5,506. Goodbody, Ernest –

P.A. Auchterturra Temperance Party.

A.S. Nil. McPherson Marilyn –

P.A. Nymphomaniac Co-operative.

A.S. Nymphomaniac fit?

P.A. Nymphomaniac Co-operative.

A.S. Nae wi' me she wisna. 343. And we ken fa they were. We ken them a'. Ritchie, Arthur.

P.A. Hands off the T.S.B.

A.S. 22. Well, he's lost his deposit. Signorini, Antonio Guiseppe –

P.A. Scottish Nationalist.

A.S. 3,312. Thomson, Alexander –

P.A. Local Greenpeacer – I'm sorry greenkeeper.

A.S. 15,580. And I declare the afore-mentioned Alexander Thomson duly elected to serve this constituency. And here he comes, folks, so let's here it for yer new M.P., Sandy Thomson. Toot-toot-toot-toot-toot-oo-roo!

(Enter Sandy Thomson, wearing an enormous rosette in Auchterturra check.)

S.T. Thank you very much ladies and gentlemen. Now, as your new M.P., it is my very pleasant duty tae mention a puckly folk that deserves a mention. And first of all I'd like tae thank the Returning Officer and his hard-working staff. Seven recounts they had. And it's nae often ye see that when there's a ten thoosand majority. But they jist had tae be sure, efter the drama o' the ballot boxes. Six extra eens turned up in an aul' press in Tullynessle School. Fortunately they were a' declared invalid, or it widna hae been me makin' this speech, it wid hiv been the late Ramsay McDonald.
Next, I would like tae thank the Police. That's Wattie Morrison, wir special fae Leochel Cushnie. Thank you Wattie. That's you lowsed now! Ye can pit awa' yer cycle clips ere the Keith Show.
Next I would like tae thank the media. That's the *Huntly Squeak*, for the

very, very fair wye they handled this election, affording equal coverage to a' the candidates. They never mentioned nane o' us. 'Cos they didna ken there was an election on. Mind you, the *Press & Journal* still disna ken.

Next, I would like tae thank the voters o' Auchterturra for turnin' oot in such force. 'Cos it couldna been a worse nicht, wi' the rival attraction o' the Family Planning Road Show – and live demonstration. Today the good people of Auchterturra have voted with their feet. 'Cos maist o' them canna write wi' their hands. And tonight the message goes out to Mrs. Thatcher: fit aboot the tax-free sharn-proof dungars for the poverty-stricken pig farmers? Get yokit, Muggie. We are fair ferfochan wi' yer flaf-fin' an' yer ficherin'.' That is the message. It could not be clearer. But yet, the besom still stubbornly pretends she doesna understand us.

Next, I would like tae thank my opponents for a good clean fecht. Except for the smear campaign against Tony the ice-creamer's knicker-bocker glory, that bides up the stair fae him. It is not true that she spent last Tues-day nicht wi' Vincent Hanna – it was Wednesday. She was wi' me on Tuesday. Finally, and on a personal note, ladies and gentlemen, I would like to thank my wife, for keepin' oot o' the bloody road!

News At Ten

A.B. Hello, Alistair Burnett here for *News at Ten*. Now, you may be suprised to see me on this programme, but this is a joint production, B.B.C. and I.T.V. We don't often co-operate, but we have to at Auchterturra, because the hall has only got one plug. However, the two channels are now separating again. On I.T.V. you can see a repeat of last night's documentary about the Aberdeenshire Police. This is at the request of the Chief Constable, because while he was on the air, somebody nicked his video. Meanwhile, on B.B.C., it's time for a last look at the weather with Ian McCaskill.

Weather Forecast

Ian McCaskill appears, flanked by a large map of the British Isles showing ominously dark rain-clouds covering Aberdeenshire.

I.M. Hello. Now it's not often that I get really excited, but tonight's By-Election result in Auchterturraturraturraturra is going to create something of a storm. That's a political storm, not a meterolololological storm which is just as well, because I can't say meterolololological. Now the weather in Auchterturraturraturra is of course dominated by an extraordinary phenomenomenon. Severe gale-force winds, very violent, very powerful, gusting in strongly. You've heard of Hurricane Hannah from the Carri-bean? This is Hurricane Beldie from Aberfeldy, producing variable patches, rather nasty variable patches, originating in *Northern* Ireland, sweeping over *Northern* England up to *Northern* Scotland. The weather in

Auchterturraturraturra never remaining the same for any length of time but switching rapidly from stair rods to dingin' doon, to nae takin' time tae come doon, to 'hale water. And the forecast tomorrow is –there could be all of these at once and there could be rain as well. So, a fairly typical fairly average summer's day in Auchterturraturraturra. Now, usually I like to finish with a summary chart but I can't do that here, because in Auchterturraturraturra the weather never is summery, it's always wintry. That's it. Good-night.

The In-Depth Interview.

A.B. Hello, Alistair Burnett here again. Since I spoke to you last, I've moved on, and I'm now speaking to you from the public bar of *The Glaikit Stirk*. It's a big night here. They've got a late licence till midnight and they'll be drinking till ten in the morning. *(Sound of piano)* As you can hear, there's a ceilidh already well under way. It's being led by a local worthy, Fobie Farquhar the flesher, and I can hear Fobie now sounding a fanfare to welcome the victor of Auchterturra, Sandy Thomson, M.P. *(Enter Sandy Thomson)*

A.B. Mr. Thomson, congratulations.

S.T. Thank you, Alistair.

A.B. Now, you and I could speak about fiscal policy, economics . . .

S.T. Well . . . maybe you could . . .

A.B. But, now that you're an M.P., what's life going to be like for you?

S.T. Bloody good! Oh, it's a great place London, ye ken!

A.B. Have you decided where you'll be staying?

S.T. Well, I thocht I'd bothy twa or three nichts at the Dorchester.

A.B. Of course, it's in the *Good Food Guide.*

S.T. Aye, five stars for stovies!

A.B. Now, what aspect of this campaign gave you most satisfaction?

S.T. The free drink! Ken this? I never had tae put my hand in my pooch.

A.B. Well of course, you are a very well-known and well-liked local figure.

S.T. Oh, but it was the same for a' the candidates. I mind ae nicht, ye ken, we had an open forum in *The Glaikit Stirk*, and a' the candidates got free beer a' nicht.

A.B. Not the temperance candidate?

S.T. No, he was on the nips! And fit a state he got in til! But mind you, fair do's, he drove hame. Oh he knockit doon twa or three folk, but they werena gan tae vote for him onywye.

A.B. Now of course, all the big guns were up from London for this By-Election. Didn't I see you speaking to Neil Kinnock?

S.T. Aye, an' I says tae him, 'Ginger', I says.

A.B. Didn't he mind being called 'Ginger'?

S.T. Well, he preferred it tae Baldy. 'Ginger', I says, 'dinna you be sae cocky.' I says. 'D'ye nae ken that there's nae sic a thing as a safe seat in Aberdeenshire?'

A.B. Did he believe you?

S.T. Aye, did he! He'd jist fa'en aff a tractor!

A.B. And I think I also saw you speaking to David Steel.

S.T. Aye, fine lad, Davie. Of course, he's got a local connection. His aul' man was a missionary. Three years in darkest Auchnagatt.

A.B. And of course, you met Mrs. Thatcher?

S.T. Oh wheesht! Oh, fit a deave o' a wumman. Puir Denis! Imagine bidin' wi' yon!

A.B. And did you meet Denis?

S.T. Aye, fine lad, Denis! Fine, hame-ower kind o' billie. I had a drink wi' him, ye ken, in *The Glaikit Stirk*, and he says tae me, 'Ow', he says, 'ow, cheers, Sandy' – spiks affa funny kind, ye ken. 'Cheers, Sandy. Here's mud in your eye'. And I says tae him' 'Cheers Denis', I says, 'here's sharn on yer beets tae you'.

A.B. And is it true that the Thatchers were staying at *The Glaikit Stirk*?

S.T. Nae jist the Thatchers, the hale jing-bang was in *the Glaikit Stirk*!

A.B. I thought there were only four bedrooms.

S.T. Fa telt ye that? There's only three! And Cyril Smith was in twa o' them.

A.B. And of course, Dr. David Owen was up?

S.T. Oh, thank God he wis!

A.B. Really, why?

S.T. The vet wis awa'. And Jim MacFarlane had a coo in calf.

A.B. And did Dr. Owen deliver it?

S.T. Aye, did he.

A.B. Did he make a good job of it?

S.T. No, he didna. But he wis better than the district nurse. The district nurse is a' richt wi' humans, but I widna let her loose on valuable livestock. And I'll tell ye somethin' else aboot that calfie that David Owen delivered. It'll aye hae a limp.

A.B. Really! To the left or to the right?

S.T. Ye ken this, the puir brute jist canna mak up its mind. Noo I'll hae tae awa' Alistair. *(Exit Sandy).*

A.B. Of course, David Owen would like to be Prime Minister. And, as Fobie will tell us, so would somebody else.

(Fobie, singing at the piano)

F.F. David Steel wid like tae be P.M.,
His party's first since Lloyd George.
Nicky Fairbairn's wedding outfit made
Him look a bit like Boy George.
But look at Tam there
In the Zircon affair –
With a zeal that never varies
Tam winna let go
So that folk say 'Hello!
Dalyell's awa' wi' the fairies.'

222

A.B. But if Tam's a bit feel
There are ithers as weel.

F.F. And the daftest o' these
Are the North-East M.P.'s.

A.B. Bert McQuarrie, Bob Hughes,

F.F. And wee Malcolm Bruce,

A.B. Gerry Malone, along with

F.F. Baith Buchanan *and* Smith

A.B. There's only one sane *(re-enter Sandy Thomson flourishing Auchterturra – check bunting)*

S.T. Sandy Thomson's the name.

ALL The rest are awa' wi' the fairies.

Plootered Roarin' fu', oot o' the game, a' tae gyte wi' drink, bleezin', mirac, stoned, guttered, plastered, stocious, stottin', blitzed, i.e. given to the occasional tipple.

Turra Coup A *Putsch* in a pocket borough.

Meryl Streep Runner-up to Rev. I.M. Jolly as T.V. Personality of the Year, 1986.

Huntly Squeak Weekly free sheet published quarterly, now incorporating the *Auchterturra Advertiser* and the *Clatt Free Press*.

Dungars Special protective trousers worn while working with natural organic effluvia.

Get yokit, Muggie Would the Rt. Hon. lady be good enough to sort herself out.

We're fair ferfochen wi' yer flaffin' an' yer ficherin' N.E. equivalent of 'Disgusted, Tunbridge Wells.'

Knickerbocker Glory Popular dish, usually kept on ice but easily warmed up.

Bothy at the Dorchester Bachelor self-catering accommodation near Hyde Park.

Pooch See Turra Coup.

Darkest Auchnagatt Emergent under-developed Fourth World community.

Fit a deave o' a wumman *Quel Horreur*! (Mitterand).

Fine hame-ower kinda billy Couthie chiel

Cyril Smith Two Liberal M.P.'s

The Auchterturra Band

The Auchterturra Scottish Country Dance Band, consisting of a pianist, an accordionist and a fiddler, are playing energetically. As they play the various dance tunes they sing along.

Reel: Kate Dalrymple

We are the band,
And we sit on the stand,
And we play Gay Gordons, Eightsome Reels and Lancers.
Folk that we meet
Ask us – why do we dae't,
And we must admit we hinna got nae answers.
Each of us is jist an or'n'ry mannie:
We're twa butchers,
I'm a jannie,
But ev'ry nicht
We moonlicht,
We're oot playin' for some
Drunken mob of Scottish country dancers.

The Dashing White Sergeant

It's a harmless hobby and it pays the rent,
And I wouldna say we're fraudulent,
But we never notify the government,
And we never tak' a cheque.
Any engagement to play that we take,
This is the only condition we make:
Just pay in cash as we are leavin' –
Fivers, please, at the end of the evenin'.
But one office party we went to,
We never knew they were the Revenue,
The fee – we spent it,
But the tax folk kent it,
And got maist o't back.

Strathspey: The Glasgow Highlanders

Think of any venue –
We have played them a',
A marquee at the Lonach
An' Findochty Fisherman's Ha'.
And though we recall
That we've enjoyed them all,
The finest dance for sure
Was the Ball o' Kirriemuir.
We only just survived
A wedding in Portree,
McGinty's meal an' ale
Far the pig gaed on the spree
But some were rough –
A fun'ral in Macduff.
A show in Sullom Voe
Wi' Calum Kennedy.

March: Kelvingrove

Twelve o'clock, and we're still sittin'
On our nerveless bums.
I am playing automatic'lly
An' sae's my chums.
I'm jist gaspin' for some booze.
Look at him – he's haein' a snooze.
But we're always ready when
The change of tempo comes.

Eightsome Reel: Deil Amang the Tailors

We're
Sittin' here
In the gear,
Fit a nicht we're haein',
Dancers birlin',
Hoochin', skirlin',
Naebody hears fit we're playin'.
There,
On the flair
Div they care
Fit it is they're daein'?
No, they dinna,
'Cos they hinna
Come tae dance.

Well,
Look at Sandy
Gettin' randy,
But he is a stupid tattie
That wee quinie
(Jean fae Rhynie)
She's a champion at karate.
Jean,
Fan Sandy started caperin',
Kicked him in his Mason's Apron.
That wis clever,
Sandy'll never
Dance again.

Scottish Waltz: Cailin Mo-Ruin-Sa

We wouldn't quarrel –
Our highlight has been
To go to Balmoral
To play for the Queen.
Together the Queen and
The Duke danced away,
The Queen doing a tango,
The Duke a strathspey.

The Queen Mum was absent –
No cause for alarms.
She'd gone to a disco
At the Invercauld Arms.
Charles and Diana
Gave the Eightsome big licks.
He wore the kilt – aye,
But she wore the briks.

Reel: Kate Dalrymple (Reprise)

One mair schottische
And we'll be aff the leash;
Jist a few mair minutes
Till the intermission.
Then tae the bar
For a nip and a jar –
Oh, there's naethin' drier
Than a dry musician.
All these rumpy-tumpy tunes – we bring them.
In one endless stream we string them.
Each one a gem,
It's a shame
There's nae words tae them.
It means that naebody can ever sing them.

The Lonach Traditional Highland Games where the athletes may not be fast, but the service in the beer tent is.

Mason's Apron Cf. The Nutcracker Suite (*This is Your Life*).

Strathspey Latin American Dance known only to the Duke of Edinburgh.

Invercauld Arms The Queen Mother's favourite howf in Braemar. 'She drinks us a' under the table', said one admiring regular.

Wedding Guests

In a church, cheerful wedding music is being played on the organ. Enter Bob, a guest at the wedding, carrying a grey topper and an order of service. He ushers in his wife, Dolly.

B.   Far dae ye want tae sit? Back row? Doon ye go then, doon ye go. That's it, in there, in there. That's it. O.K.? O.K.? Can ye see a' richt? Eh? Fit wifie's hat? Oh aye, weel move up, move up. *(They move along one seat)* That's it. That's it. Now, oh! There's Stan and Nora. Here, they've gone tae the wrang side. Ha ha. *(He shouts)* Stan! Stan! Ye're at the wrang side! This is the bride's side! Move over, move over. No, no. Ye've got tae move. Nora, get him ower, get him ower! Typical Stan, aye makin' a feel o' himsel in public.

(Enter Sandy, another guest. He sits beside Bob)

S. Aye, aye, Bob. Prefer this tae the golf, then?

B. Hello, Sandy. How ye doin'?

S. Nae bad. Could be daein' withoot this lot, though. An affa shame aboot the weather. Fit a waste o' a fine day.

B. Sandy, have ye met Dolly? Have ye met the wife?

S. Pleased tae meet ye, Dolly.

B. Is Betty nae wi' ye?

S. No, she's in the hospital, wi' her legs.

B. Baith o' them?

S. Aye.

B. *(Turning to Dolly)* Sandy's wife's in the hospital – wi' baith her legs. *(Turning again to Sandy)* Fa is it you ken? Div ye see Stan an' Nora?

S. Oh, aye.

B. They went tae the wrang side. This is the bride's side, and that's the groom's side. Fa's side are you on?

S. I dinnae ken. We dinna like ony o' them.

B. Fit wye did they hae it in this kirk?

S. Desperation. They tried a' wye. They went a' roon the toon. This is the only boy that wid tak them on. I think he wis desperate an' a'.

B. It's a nice enough kirk, though. I like the religious touches.

S. I think I mind bein' at a christenin' in this kirk. Little Colin Sutherland, mind?

B. Little Colin! He must be nearly thirty noo. Fit happened tae Colin?

S. Oh, his folk are affa prood o' him. He's jist got remission for good conduct.

B. Colin's folk are here. They came in wi' the Andersons in front o' us.

S. Oh, aye. Fit Andersons is that now?

B. Tommy Anderson. He's got his ain slater's business. Ye often see him on folks' roofs. But he disna jist dae slates, he does chimneys as weel.

S. Oh, hoo hoo, that must hae been him I saw cairryin' a lum hat.

B. Hey, Dolly, Dolly. Sandy has jist said, he saw Tommy Anderson, the slater, cairryin' a lum hat. Ha ha ha . . . Oh, never mind!

S. Oh me, here's the Johnstons, wi' a hale squad o' bairns. I canna be daein' wi' bairns at weddin's.

B. No. But I believe een o' the Johnston girlies is a lovely dancer. Little Maisie, is it? Fit een's she?

S. She's the een bla'in' oot the bubble gum. Oh, me, it's exploded. A' ower her face an' doon her frocky. An' her Ma's jist gien her a clout across the lug. Oh, they're real charmers, the Johnstons.

B. D'ye see that couple ower there, at the end o' the row? That's the bridegroom's uncle and auntie fae Vancouver. They flew in yesterday. He's a mountie.

S. And he's jist come straight fae his work. Aha! That must be his horse ootside, tied tae the wayside pulpit.

B. D'ye ken fa I've been lookin' for, and I canna find her onwye? Grannie Tough.

S. Grannie Tough's nae comin'.

B. Nae comin'?

S. Grannie Tough hisna been past the front door since her ninetieth birthday.

B. Aw.

S. No, it's a' richt. The happy couple have promised to pop in an' see Grannie on their wye tae the reception

B. Very nice. Far dis she bide?

S. Ballater.

B. God, we winna get wir denner till six o'clock! I'm gan tae be starvin'.

S. You should've been like Tommy Anderson. See that lum hat o' his? It's full o' sandwiches.

B. I think I've been in this kirk afore as weel. I recognise that stained glass windae. I mean, fa is that?

S. That's Jesus.

B. There ye go. I kent it rang a bell. Oh, there's Jessie Laing.

S. Jessie Laing? Fit Jessie Laing's that now?

B. Div ye nae ken Jethie Laing that thpiks like thith . . . I'll tell ye, wi' Betty nae bein' here, you'll maybe get Jethie Laing for yer partner.

S. I'm nae wantin' nae partner. And I'm certainly nae wantin' Jethie Laing that thpiks like this. I'm jist here for a return on wir investment. Forty quid we spent on a present.

B. Forty quid! That's gan ower the score a bittie intit? If ye dinna like the folk . . . Or even if ye div like the folk.

S. But we got it wholesale.

B. Ah!

S. It costs seventy quid in the shops!

B. Ah, but you're still forty quid oot o' pocket!

S. Ah, but they'll think we're seventy quid oot o' pocket. And it is the thought that counts.

B. Eh? Ah, Dolly's just reminded me, we gave them a set o' fish knives and forks. We've been to fower weddings this year and we gave them a' fish knives and forks.

S. Fit wye did ye gie a'body fish knives an' forks?

B. 'Cos a' body gave *us* fish knives and forks. We've got a hale cupboard full o' fish knives and forks.

S. Weel, I just hope that the bridegroom likes fish. 'Cos the bride certainly disna.

B. Celia? Does she nae?

S. Oh no, ony kind o' fish – she comes oot in a rash.

B. A rash?

S. Aye, her face, ken? Blotches. Lumps, ken? Half a sardine an' she's like the Elephant Man. So quite honestly Bob, I canna see them makin' much use o' yer fish knives and forks. Never mind, they can aye gie them awa' as a wedding present.

B. Well, that would be a poor show! Efter a' that trouble we went till gettin' them oot o' the cupboard.

S. Here, dae ye like yer fancy programme? It's just swank that. That is Ethel a' ower.

B. Absolutely! Twenty years Ethel's been waitin' tae be mither o' the bride. And this is gan tae be her day . . . Oh me! Here she comes.

S. In full sail! Fit a track! Spik aboot mutton . . . dressed as mock chop!

B. Tell me, is Ethel happy enough wi' the bridegroom? Fit's his name – Barry? I mean, does she think he's good enough for Celia?

S. Well, beggars canna be choosers, can they? Have ye seen Celia?

B. Nae lately, no, but I believe she's got a very sweet nature.

S. Oh, she would need tae hae. Oh, she's nae bonny. Mind you, last time I saw her, she'd just had yalla fish for her tea.

B. Fit aboot the bridegroom's folk? Fit dae we ken aboot them?

S. They're a bit o' a mystery. There's some word aboot them bein' separated.

B. Oh, they are separated. Apparently it was a very stormy marriage.

S. A love hate relationship?

B. No, just hate. Apparently they were aye fechtin'. Shoutin' an' sweirin'. Throwin' things. Windaes wis broken. The bobbies wis up an' a' thing. They jist bade thegither for Barry's sake. Tae mak sure he had a settled upbringin', ken? That must be them in the front row!

S. Here, there's fower folk there, Bob . . . .

B. Aye, Dolly's got it a' worked oot. Ye see the wifie in the reid white an' blue?

S. Oh aye. Reid frock, white hat an' blue rinse.

B. Well that's Barry's mither.

S. That's the mither!

B. Aye, that's the mither. An' the fat boy, see the fat boy?

S. Oh aye. Morning suit, and he's got bad feet.

B. Foo dae ye ken he's got bad feet?

S. He's wearin' Jimmies.

B. Well, that's Barry's faither.

S. That's the faither.

B. Aye, that's the faither. And the baldy mannie in the kilt is the boyfriend.

S. Barry's faither's boyfriend?

B. No no, Barry's mither's boyfriend . . . And the dolly bird in the fur coat and the fancy jewellery is Barry's faither's personal physiotherapist. Fit a set-up.

S. Fit a set-up! Oh, I dinna ken aboot you Bob, but seein' that kind o' thing really upsets me, that!

B. Seein' that marriages can brak up?

S. Naw, seein' a fat mannie twice my age wi' a fancy bit o' stuff like that.

B. Oh, here's Barry and the best man! Oh, they're baith in the kilt. Very good!

S. I believe the best man wisna affa keen on wearin' the kilt . . . bein' a Sikh, ken?

B. Well I'll tell ye, it disna ging wi' his turban! Could they nae get him a Glengarry? Ha ha.

S. Or a lum hat, ha ha.

B. Full o' sandwiches. Ha ha.

(We hear the introduction to the Bridal March)

S. Oh, here we go.

B. Here we go.

(They stand and smile to the bride as she passes them. Then they exchange meaningful glances)

S. Did you see fit I saw? Puir lassie! On her wedding day. She shouldna have had a kipper for her breakfast.

Jimmies Designer footwear worn by the young when in the gym and the old when in discomfort.

Track Expensive ticket (see *Welcome to the World's Bowlers*)

'YOUNGER THAN US'

Regretfully, ♩ = 69

They say if the bobby on the beat looks young, it's the first sign you're gettin' aul'_____. jist a-boot a' bo-dy I meet looks young, which is nae good for my mo——rale_____. Pro—fessors & physicians, a're—sponsible po-si—tions, It's youngsters fa—re-ver I see_____. It's nae jist p'lice constables, E—ven Chief Constables, They're a' younger than me, and me, and me, and thus, They're a' younger than

colla voce

a tempo

us. If I ging tae the quack wi' my si-nus or my back, The doc tor's jist a young loon. If I'm at a re-qui-em in a kirk or at the crem, The mi-ni-ster's jist a young loon_____. Art gal-le-ry Di-rec-tor & the Sa-ni-t'ry Inspector & the boy who drives the Mannofield bus. All ac——countants pale & wee-dy, & the Gordon's College Heidie They're a' younger than us. 2. If the us.

Younger than us are _____ all these, And the vast bulk of _____ M.— P.'s But

What we most hate is the Secret'ry of State is Youn — ger too.

rit. , D.S.

Bob—by

CODA

tempo

Charl-ton, Kevin Keegan, Well a—part fae Ronald Reagan. A—bo-dy's younger than The I—talian in his ca-fé is

rit _ (molto) _ _ _ tempo (jauntily)

Colonel mad Gadaffi is, Each painter & each plumber is, the So-vi-et heid bummer is A'bo dy's younger than us.

rit _ (molto) _ _ _ tempo

Younger Than Us

They say, if the bobby on the beat looks young,
It's the first sign *you're* gettin' aul',
But jist aboot a'body I meet looks young,
Which is nae good for my morale.
Professors and physicians – a' responsible positions –
It's youngsters farever I see.
It's nae jist p'lice constables,
Even Chief Constables,
They're a' younger than me
                and me
                and me,
                and thus
They're a' younger than us.

If I ging tae the quack wi' my sinus or my back,
The doctor's jist a young loon.
If I'm at a requiem in a kirk or at the crem,
The minister's jist a young loon.
Art Gallery Director and the sanit'ry inspector
And the boy that drives the Mannofield bus,
All accountants pale and weedy, and the Gordon's College heidie,
They're a' younger than us.

If the bairn's nae daein' weel, an' I'm summoned tae the squeel,
The teacher's jist a young quine.
If my Ma's feelin' worse, and I get the District Nurse,
Fan she comes she's jist a young quine.
My Auntie Nell's health visitor, my dentist, my solicitor
The wifie in the Co-opie mak'n a fuss,
Every pundit on the telly, Rajiv Gandhi ow'r in Delhi,
They're a' younger than us.

Younger than us are all these,
And the vast bulk of M.P.'s,
But what we most hate is
The Secret'ry of State is
Younger too.

If, financially sunk, I totter tae the bunk,
The manager's jist a young loon.
Fan I pit the bucket oot, an' the lorry gies a toot,
God! the scaffie's jist a young loon.
And I have a firm impression, a' the medical profession –
Like the mannie that I went til for my truss,
Ev'ry prosp'rous licensed victualler – neen o' them remembers Hitler –
They're a' younger than us.

It really maks me wince fan I buy a pun' o' mince,
'Cos the butcher's jist a young loon.
In the past the folk said 'Sir' to the Dons' manager,
But Fergie's jist a young loon.
The surgeons at the clinic, David Owen, Neil Kinnock,
A' the folk the Sunday papers discuss,
Bobby Charlton, Kevin Keegan –
Well, apart fac Ronald Reagan,
A'body's younger than us.

Fergie   Duchess of York (cf Katie Rabbit and Koo in *The Moderator*).

At the Assembly

Hamish, a minister, is sitting on a bench in Princes Street Gardens. Archie, an old minister (who as a former Moderator, delivered the sermon at Crathie Kirk), wearing a knotted handkerchief on his head, is feeding the pigeons from a small paper bag. Hamish rises from the bench and approaches him.

H.   Hello, Archie.

A.   Hello, Hamish. My goodness, what a fright you gave me. I've just been for my lunch.

H.   I was wondering where I would go for my own lunch. There's a little place I like the look of just off the Royal Mile. A Chinese trattoria. But I hear it's very pricey.

A.   So? Get a receipt. Put it through your expenses.

H.   Oh, I don't think my treasurer would wear that.

A.   Oh? Who is your treasurer?

H.   He's the local bank manager.

A.   That's your first mistake. Bank managers are fine enough, but nae as kirk treasurers. Ye're much better aff wi' a publican. Especially if he's a sinner as well.

H.   Oh, I'm a complete innocent in financial matters. My thoughts tend to be on more spiritual things.

A.   Oh, I'm happy enough aboot eternity. It's my retirement I'm worried aboot. And that stipend they pay us nowadays –

H.   Quite, quite. You know, we'd be much better off in the Church of England. A cousin of mine went into the Church of England. He was a bishop by the time he was forty. Of course he was a very good cricketer. Like David Sheppard. He played at Lord's with Sheppard.

A.   Ah! My favourite psalm, Hamish.

H.   What!

A.   *The Lord's my Shepherd.*

H. Well, as you know, Archie, I got a distinction in New Testament Greek, but that flannelled fool of a cousin of mine is making a lot more money than I am.

A. Now, now, Hamish, thou shalt not covet thy neighbour's pay packet. That's the way of the world these days. You've got to go to England for the big money. Alex Ferguson did the same.

H. *(Earnestly changing the subject)* I think it's been a very good Assembly this year, very stimulating, don't you?

A. I wouldna know. I hinna been near the place. Not since the High Commissioner's cocktail party the nicht afore it started.

H. I wasn't at the cocktail party.

A. Oh, but you should have gone, Hamish.

H. No, no. I wasn't invited.

A. Oh, but neither was I. I just swicked in. When you've got on a dog collar you can get away with murder.

H. Well, you've been missing some excellent speeches this year.

A. Listen to me, Hamish. When you've been in this game as lang as I have there's nae much ye hinna heard afore.

H. But some of the new young men have been very good.

A. Oh, dinna spik tae me aboot the young brigade. Stirring things up. Wearing a collar and tie, some of them. Instead of a dog collar. What kind of way's that for a minister to go about? Where I come from a minister is supposed to look like a minister . . . . . .

(At this Hamish has a good look at his companion and registers expressively his disapproval of the bizarre picture he presents.)

A. . . . . . and not skulk about in disguise. Do you know, Hamish, there's a young minister living in my hotel and he wears a T-shirt – with writing across the front.

H. 'Praise the Lord'?

A. 'Frankie goes to Hollywood'.

H. So have you not been at any of the formal sessions at all?

A. None of the plenary ones. The only thing I've been at was a working party on stipends and allowances. It was at the Caledonian Hotel, and there was a cup of tea and a sausage roll.

H. I'm sorry I missed that one.

A. Yes, it was affa fine flaky pastry.

H. Well, you've been missing some very good stuff, you know. Yesterday's debate on ethics and morality.

A. Oh, I heard a bit o' that. I was out at my sister's at Portobello for my supper – she does a very nice chocolate sponge – and I saw it on the T.V.

H. Of course. They do recorded highlights of the Assembly, late at night.

A. That's right. Efter the snooker. Or I wouldna hiv kent it was on.

H. Did you manage to catch Willie Duncan from Inverness? Willie spoke very well on The Seven Deadly Sins.

A. I'm nae surprised. He's tried maist o' them. No, no. I dinna care much for Willie Duncan. That Mary Marquis, now, that he was spikkin' til at the end o' the programme – what a rare bit o' stuff. I wish she had been around in my day. What a rare minister's wife she would have made. Instead of that battle-axe I got stuck wi'.

H. I think you're being a bit hard on Willie Duncan.

A. Oh, dinna spik tae me aboot Willie Duncan. Goodness, I've kent Willie a' my days. We were students together at Aberdeen University, and what a wild, spilt loon he wis. His aul' man had pots of money, and Willie used to drive about in this aul' banger o' a car. Well, one Saturday night some of us divinity chaps had been at the hop – and nae luck as usual – and Willie was driving us home to wir digs in the Y.M.C.A. Well, Willie had had a fair drink, and the car was waving about, and we were stopped by the police, and we'd got to go to Lodge Walk. Well, the bobby says tae Willie, 'Young man,' he says, 'walk along that white line, stand on one leg and pick up that half crown.' And Willie says, 'Dinna be stupid, constable,' he says, can you not see I'm pissed.'*(The shock brought on by the climax of this narrative causes Hamish to clutch his heart and to steady himself by resting his other hand on Archie's shoulder.)* Well, he was clapped into jail straight away.

H. For drunk driving?

A. Foul language. Quite right too.

H. I see quite a lot of Willie Duncan these days. On charity things. Willie's on every charity committee you can think of.

A. Oh, aye. He's a terrible do-gooder. It's pathetic. You'd think he'd hae better things tae dae wi' his time. Well, well, but it's up to him – as lang as he disna try tae ram it doon ither folk's throats. No, no. I've got enough to do with my own congregation.

H. What size of flock do you have?

A. It's funny you should say that. I do have more sheep than folk.

H. Where exactly is your parish?

A. Nowheresville. I've got a cushie wee number at the back of beyond, but I'm not tellin' you or anybody else where it is. *(He opens his jacket to reveal what by this stage the audience knows to be an Auchterturra waistcoat.)* But verily hath the Lord bestowed his blessing in abundance on his humble servant.

H. I must say, it sounds idyllic.

A. Oh, yes. Of a summer evening, I step out into my back garden, stroll down the path, sweet peas on my left, a clump of lupins and my bird bath on my right – I like watchin' the blackies haein' a dook – I walk down the path, past my lawn and the soft fruit, and down to an old stone wall at the bottom. I open the gate in the wall – it creaks a bittie, it's needin' ilin' – push aside a rambling rose, go through the gate, and I'm straight into the back door of the distillery. Idyllic, as you say.

H. I'm speaking myself in tomorrow's debate on falling attendances in the kirk. Are you going to that one?

A. No, I'm going to the Zoo tomorrow morning.

H. No, no, this is in the afternoon.

A. Oh, I'm going to the picters in the afternoon.

H. Ah, with the Special Study Group.

A. That's right. We're going to see a religious film in Cinema 2.

H. What's it called?

A. Emanuelle 3. That's the trouble with Edinburgh at Assembly time. There's so much to do. If it's not the Zoo or the picters, it's sherry parties, tea parties, friends to look up, relatives to visit – it's a great place Edinburgh at Assembly time. There's only one thing wrong with it, and there's no answer to it that I can see.

H. What's that?

A. The hale place is jist hotchin' wi' Holy Willies.

David Sheppard Father of Robbie (q.v.)

Frankie Goes to Hollywood A little-known text from Deuteronomy.

Mary Marquis Pin-up girl of Aberdeen University Divinity Faculty Alumni.

Hop Saturday evenings excuse (with music) for meeting birds (note Archie's affinity with St. Francis of Assissi) after tanking up.

Lodge Walk Sometime nerve-centre of the battle against crime in Aberdeen. Now closed (cf. Cinemas, Chip Shops etc.).

Blackies haein' a dook Blackbirds enjoying an ornithological jacuzzi – further evidence of Archie's bird fixation.

'TRIVIAL PURSUIT'

doesn't matter Oe-di-pus was chummy with his Mummy, Who cares if a to-ma-to is a veg'ta-ble or fruit? It

on-ly matters if you're playin' Trivi-al Pursuit.

Who

cares if a-tom bombs go off if ye leave them a-boot? Well, that wid fairly stop ye playin' Tri-vi-al Pursuit!

Trivial Pursuit

There's a craze these days that's bordering on hysteria,
A board game that has caused a great hubbub,
But I find that it makes me feel inferior,
So if you feel the same, folks, join the club.

It can be quite convivial
Tae play at Trivial
Pursuit,
But if you never dae weel at a'
You shouldna feel at a'
Pit oot.
'Cos it doesn't matter really which is Scotland's smallest county,
Or who it was played Captain Bligh in *Mutiny on the Bounty,*
It doesn't matter Harpo was the Marx who was the dummy,
It doesn't matter Oedipus was chummy with his mummy,
Who cares if a tomato is a veg'table or fruit?
It only matters if you're playing Trivial Pursuit.

Who cares where Whistler's Mum was found?
Or when Columbus found
The States?
For most folk it's irrelevant
How long an elephant
Gestates.
It doesn't matter what the function of your chromosomes is
It doesn't matter Watson was a chum of Sherlock Holmes's
It doesn't matter that it was James Joyce who wrote *Ulysses*
It doesn't matter Anne Boleyn was Henry's second missus
Who cares if, when the tide came in, it drookit King Canute
It only matters if you're playing Trivial Pursuit.

You're stuck if there's a query on
Something Shakespearean –
So what?
Who invented electricity?
Important? Is it, eh?
It's not!
And it doesn't matter Paris thought that Helen of Troy was gorgeous,
It doesn't matter no-one liked a bevy with the Borgias,
It doesn't matter who invented general anaesthesia,
It doesn't matter if Yul Brynner did have alopecia.
Who cares if Biggles ever flew without a parachute?
It only matters if you're playing Trivial Pursuit.

Did Kellog first make cereal?
It's immaterial
To me.
It matters not a jot to me
What a lobotomy
Might be.
It doesn't matter where you'd go to see the Mona Lisa,
Or how far off the plumb you'd find the Leaning Tower of Pisa;
It doesn't matter what the language is in Venezuela,
Or if the dying Nelson said to Hardy, 'Hello, sailor.'
Who cares if Gerald Ford got in when Nixon was kicked oot?
It only matters if you're playing Trivial Pursuit.

A question asked quite often is:
Name Aristophanes'
First play.
To which an answer never comes
If that one ever comes
My way.
It doesn't really matter whose last words were, *'Et tu, Brute.'*
Or how old Mozart was when he composed *Cosi Fan Tutte*
It doesn't matter H$_2$O's the formula for water,
It doesn't matter if Princess Di is Marks' or Spencer's daughter.
Who cares if atom bombs go off if ye leave them lyin' aboot?
Well, that wid fairly stop ye playin' Trivial Pursuit!

Drookit Consequence of ill-advised or reckless pleiterin' (q.v.) A theory that the king was drunk
at the time is borne out by the recent discovery of a fragment of 11th century manuscript containing the barely legible inscription 'p....d as Canute'.

The Stop-Go Man

Mr. Wallace is discovered holding a Stop-Go sign and yawning. Enter Mr Taylor, wearing a peaked cap and carrying a 'Children Crossing' sign.

T.   Toot, toot!

W.   *(Turning his sign appropriately.)* Stop!

T.   Stop?

W.   Aye, stop.

T.   Fit d'ye mean, stop?

W.   Jist fit I say, stop.

T.   You canna stop me. I'm nae a car.

W.   I can stop onybody I like. I can stop onybody I dinna like. I stopped a fire engine yesterday. Fit a speed it wis gan. Lights flashin', bells ringin'. I says tae the boy, 'Hey, min! Far's the fire?' He wisna pleased.

T.   But that wis yesterday.

W.   That wis yesterday.

T.   Fit aboot the day? Hiv ye been busy?

W.   Busy? Gee whiz!

T.   Dinna ken fit wye tae turn, eh? Ha ha!

W.   Oh, I ken fit wye tae turn. 'Go', fan I want them tae go. And 'Stop', fan I want them tae stop.

T.   Very good. 'Cos I didna think ye were gan tae get the hang o't.

W.   Neither did I!

T.   'Cos ye never got the hang o' bein' a lollipop man. Safety first, O.K. There wis some days 'at bairns never got intae the school at a'.

W.   Well, the bairns werna complainin'.

T. An' I hope ye're lookin' efter 'at sign. It's a valuable piece of equipment, that sign. Wi' the money they peyed oot on 'at sign, the Regional Cooncil could've employed three teachers.

W. Awa' ye go!

T. I'm tellin' ye. It wis either that or sign three new guidance teachers for Auchterturra Primary.

W. Awa' ye go. I wis a year at Auchterturra Primary an' I never got nae guidance.

T. Of course ye didna. 'At wis the year they bocht 'at Stop-Go sign.

W. Ken 'is Mr. Taylor. I think you're jist jealous. Me gettin' this job efter you pit in for it.

T. Oh, I kent I hadna got it. I made an affa mess o' my interview.

W. Oh, yon interview is an affa ordeal. Gan intae that big room an' seein' the hale Regional Cooncil sittin' roon the table looking at ye.

T. Aye. Some o' that boys will dae onything for attendance money. Onywye, the very first thing they asked me – I wis oot o' the game.

W. Fit wis it?

T. My name and address.

W. I ken. Yer mind jist gings a complete blank, dis it?

T. Aye. but I kent it. I did ken it. It wis on the tip o' my tongue, but could I get it oot?

W. I ken. It's nae fair. At the very start. A trick question.

T. I ken. But the next thing they asked me really finished me. Well, the chairman boy, the Regional Convenor –

W. The boy wi' the beard an' the bike?

T. That's him. He says tae me, he says, 'Who in your opinion has made the biggest contribution to the efficient running of Grampian Region?' Well, I didna hear him right, and I says, 'Sorry?'

W. An' fit did he say?

T. 'Oot!' But I suppose you'd a good interview, had ye?

W. Oh aye. Pretty good. Well, I'm at my best in an interview situation.

T. Fit's yer secret?

W. Personal charisma. I jist let my personality shine through.

T. So is that fit got ye this job?

W. Well, that, an my uncle Bill's the gaffer.

T. Aye, aye. It's nae fit ye ken, it's fa ye ken. 'At's jist nepotism, 'at.

W. Ne-pot-ism? Fit's a nepot?

T. Well, yer uncle Bill that got ye that job. He's a nepot.

W. I never kent my uncle Bill wis a nepot. I kent he wis a mason.

T. Well, it's pretty sickenin'. I wis really cut up aboot nae gettin' that job.

252

W. But I thocht ye liked bein' a lollipop man?

T. Well, I used til. But these days, there's a lot o's in education is pretty dis-enchanted. In fact we're nae pleased at a'. But enough aboot me. Fit aboot yersel'? Foo mony vehicles have ye controlled this mornin'?

W. Well, I've had twa cars an' a tractor an' a boy on a bike.

T. So that's fower vehicles atween 8 o'clock and 1 o'clock.

W. Aye, but nae every day's the same. Yesterday wisna nearly sae busy.

T. Fower vehicles in a hale mornin'. Fit ye been daein' the rest o' the time?

W. I've been thinkin'.

T. Oh aye. Fit aboot? Einstein's Theory o' Relativity?

W. No. Nae this mornin'. Ye can get fed up wi' Einstein, can ye? He wis a clever enough bloke, it's jist a peety he didna hit it aff wi' Monty.

T. Hit it aff wi' Monty? You're thinkin' o' Eisenhower.

W. Oh, 'at's richt. Eisenhower's Theory o' Relativity.

T. Come on, then. Fit is the Theory o' Relativity?

W. Well, it's a theory. Aboot yer relatives. Like – if ye want a cushie job, mak sure yer uncle's the gaffer.

T. So fit *hiv* ye been thinkin' aboot?

W. I've been thinkin' aboot fit I wid dae if I won the pools.

T. Oh, aye. Fit wid ye dae? Wid ye gie up this job?

W. Oh no! I widna ken fit tae dae wi' mysel'. I wid jist be sittin' at hame daein' naething.

T. Well, it wid mak a change fae standin' aboot here daein naething. A hale morning – fower vehicles.

W. Did I say fower? I've jist minded something else. But I dinna ken if it coonts.

T.   Fit wis it?

W.   A coo. Dis a coo coont?

T.   Dis a coo coont? No, I've never seen a coo coontin'. It hisna got enough fingers.

W.   Then efter the coo a puckly sheep went through.

T.   Sheep?

W.   Aye, sheep. Like little coos wi woolly jumpers.

T.   Foo mony sheep?

W.   I'm nae sure.

T.   Did ye nae coont them?

W. Aye, but fan I got up tae eleven I fell asleep.

T. Oh, gee! Some mothers do have them!

W. Did you ken my mither?

T. Did I ken your mither? – Did you ken that afore your mither got merried she used tae ging wi' my aul' man. Then they went tae the Palais ae nicht an' your aul' man moved in an' cut the feet.

W. 'At's richt. He chatted her up at the bar. Then he offered her a puff o' his Capstan Full Strength.

T. An' 'at wis it?

W. 'At wis it. They jist seemed tae hit it aff.

T. Ah yes. A chance meeting at the Palais de Dance. A shared taste for Capstan Full Strength. On such slender threads, Mr Wallace, do our destinies hang. We're back tae the Theory of Relativity again. Except it's yer mither an' yer faither this time. If they hidna met that nicht, you widna be here the day.

W. Wid I nae? Far wid I be?

T. No, no. Fit I'm sayin' is – if your mither hidna merried yer faither you widna be here at a'.

W. Aye, I wid. I wis six year aul' afore they got married.

Hey, min Form of address to strangers in Aberdeen (cf. 'Ye're a stranger' in *Arrival*), courteous to the point of sycophancy.

The boy wi' the beard 'an the bike The new Convenor of Grampian Region kept his beard, but gave up his bike when the Council's chauffeur declined to switch from a Daimler to a tandem.

Sorry? A misguided attempt at politeness. He would have been better simply saying, 'Fit? Spik up, beardie' to the new Convenor whose predecessor's name was Sorrie.

Eisenhower Distinguished American physicist and golfer, not to be confused with the English sculptor or Russian film director of the same name.

Capstan Full Strength Fashionable narcotic (with aphrodisical properties) in the 1930's.

Small Hotel

Tune: *There's a Small Hotel*

Show business is all right, sweetheart,
But there are drawbacks too:
Often I spend the night, sweetheart,
Miles away from you.

Of all the places I stay, sweetheart,
Some quite unknown, some quite renowned,
I'm writing now to-day, sweetheart,
To let you know that here I've found
The worst one . . .

There's a small hotel
Outside Motherwell,
It's hell
No matter what the weather.
Mattress like a brick,
Spotty candlewick,
A pair of sheets that stick
Together.

Breakfast in the morning –
There is porridge on and coffee,
Porridge is like toffee,
Coffee's – awfie.

The staff's a surly crew,
And it's pricy too –
The owner drives a new
Mercedes.
Lounge for residents –
Used with diffidence –
It's right above the Gents
And Ladies.

Looking for a window,
I assume the room has got one.
But I cannot spot one,
'Cos there's not one.

But it's just one day,
Then I get away.
My stay
Could not have been much worse, so
Goodbye small hotel,
Goodbye dingy cell,
Farewell that funny smell.
To-morrow I leave Motherwell,
And then I have a nice short drive
To Thurso.

The Dinner Dance

The scene is the company dinner dance. The Chairman (Basil) and the Managing Director (Henry), wearing paper hats are seated at a table. Basil's wife Audrey and Henry's wife Daphne sit opposite their husbands. Basil blows a novelty tooteroo.

H.   A brandy with your coffee, Basil?

B.   Aye, to wash down my double whisky.

H.   Sorry girls, what about a wee liqueur? Audrey? Daphne? Waiter, could we have a Benedictine, a Cointreau, a brandy and – och, I'll just have a half-pint – of Drambuie shandy. *(He feels for his wallet)*

B.   Here, put it away. Let me get this one. You got the cloakroom tickets.

H.   So I did. Thanks very much.

(Basil blows his tooteroo again)

B.   Here, listen to this, Daphne. *(He blows again)* Name that tune. Now, here's one for you, Henry. It's an impression, this time. *(He gives a short toot, then mopping his brow with his handkerchief he sings in a voice approximating to Louis Armstrong's)* 'Well, hello, Dolly –'

H.   Basil, I've no idea.

B.   James Galway.

H.   Oh, here comes the coffee. Thank you very much. Just put it down there. Oh, splendid. You get mints as well.

B.   Mince? Is there a mealie pudding with it?

H.   No, no, Basil. After Eight Mints.

B.   Oh, that kind of mints. Oh! Look out Daphne, you're about to drop a bit of chocolate down your front. Oops! Too late. It's away.

H.   What, dear? You want to go to the cloakroom and have a go at retrieving it? Of course.

(Basil and Henry stand)

B.   Audrey, you go with her and give her a hand. I think you'll find a couple

of Brussels sprouts down there as well. And a melon boat.

H.   I must say, all the staff seem to be enjoying themselves.

B.   Aye. I like seeing all the girlies in their pretty frocks. Have you seen Morag from despatch?

H.   I don't think I would know Morag. I don't see much of her during the year.

B.   Well, you'll see a lot of her tonight!

H.   You'd better simmer down, and get the raffle going.

B.   Is it raffle time? *(He lurches to his feet)* Settle down, ladies and gentlemen, it's raffle time. We'll draw the prizes in reverse order. And the third prize is a bottle of Brut Aftershave. And the winning number, Henry, is –?

H.   *(Drawing a ticket from his hat)* Pink 86.

B.   Pink 86, pink 86, who's won the Brut Aftershave? Miss Cruickshank. Miss Foosty Cruickshank. Never mind, Miss Cruickshank. You will look more like Henry Cooper than ever now. Now the second prize is a £5 gift voucher for Boot's the Chemist. And the winning number is –

H. Green 37.

B. Green 37. Dougie Smith from the warehouse. Well, Dougie, if all I hear about you is correct, that won't keep you going for very long. Is that not right, girls? Now finally, this year's star prize is a lovely water-colour painting, 'Reclining Nude at Pittodrie', and it's been very kindly donated by my good friend, Henry here. Where did you get it, Henry?

H. I won it in last year's raffle.

B. Oh, so you did. Well the winning number this year is –

H. Green 104.

B. Green 104. Come on, own up, someone must have it. Green 104.

H. I've won the bloody thing again!

B. Congratulations, Henry. Well now, it's on with the dancing, and it's over to Aberdeen's best-known group, Boomtown Mouse. *(The band play Paul Jones).* Oh, it's a Paul Jones. Come on Henry. We'll have to show the flag.

H. I can't do a Paul Jones. I don't know the steps.

(By this time they are on the dance floor and they do a Paul Jones, obviously as part of a large circle. Then for the first dance, an old-fashioned waltz. Henry is obviously partnered by a small lady, Basil by a tall one. Their conversation is overheard.)

B. Your face is familiar. I'm sure I've seen you somewhere before, Haven't I? Oh, you're a secretary. Very nice. Oh, you're *my* secretary!

H. So you work in despatch ? Morag isn't it? Do you enjoy it in despatch? You enjoy it anywhere.

B. Where are you going for your holidays? Crete? Very nice. Tell me, do girls go topless in Crete? What? Oh, not Crete – Crieff. Good grief!

H. Do they keep you busy in despatch, Morag? What? Some nights you have to work late? Well, if I can give you a lift home – No, no trouble at all. I often go home to Stonehaven via Peterhead.

(The band resumes the Paul Jones music and the two men make their way back to their seats.)

H. That'll do me. I'm not as fit as I was.

B. Aye, it's a young man's game, that. Here, we've got some very important guests tonight. That's Tommy Calder, the surgeon.

H. Don't remind me. I'm going into dock next week for a gall bladder thing. Tommy's doing the op.

B. Goodness, I was playing golf with Tommy just last Monday.

H. He's a very fine golfer, Tommy.

B. Oh, he's a very fine golfer. If he was half as good with his scalpel as he is with his No. 5 iron, you'd be in with a fighting chance.

H. And at the same table, that's Tommy's brother, Peter. He's one of these criminal lawyers.

B. Criminal lawyers? Jolly difficult to find one who isn't.

H. And there's Graeme Souness, the Rangers manager. That was a good move of his signing Butcher.

B. Och, he's not the first butcher to play for Rangers.

H. Rangers will be looking forward to playing in Europe next season.

B. Oh, no. Haven't you heard? They've been banned.

H. Banned?

B. Aye, like all the other English clubs. Oh, look, there's that big farmer chap, Sir Maitland Mackie.

H. Is he a guest?

B. No, he's come to deliver the milk.

H. You know, I agree with you. There's some very attractive women here tonight. But there's none of them looking as nice as your Audrey.

B. Yes, Audrey is looking nice. do you like her new contact lenses?

H. Is she wearing contact lenses? I never noticed them behind her specs.

B. And your Daphne's looking super. That's a very fetching pair of culottes she's wearing.

H. Aye, she got them through a clubbie book. You wouldn't get a thing like that from a shop.

B. No, I don't suppose you would. Not unless it was Hall Russell's.

H. Don't you think Daphne's rather a nifty dancer?

B. She is. She's very light on her feet for such a – how heavy is Daphne these days?

H. She's down to sixteen stone. Well, last week I took her out to dinner – collected her after her Weight Watchers, picked her up in the horse box. We went to the Holiday Inn Hotel.

B. Oh yes. That's the place where they've got the super swimming pool.

H. Well, they did have before Daphne dived into it after two helpings of Clootie Dumpling. *(The band begins to play* Auld Lang Syne.*)* Now what's that they're playing?

B. It's a Pas a Doble.

H. A Pas a Doble! It's *Auld Lang Syne.* Come on.

(They are in time to join in (with crossed arms) the final lines of Auld Lang Syne. *At the end of it, Basil calls for three cheers, then the band plays* For He's a Jolly Good Fellow *and Basil pushes an unwilling Henry into the middle of the company.)*

H. Thank you very much. We've had a wonderful evening. Good night. God bless. And a safe journey home. I'll be all right. I don't have the car this evening. I'm getting a lift home from my good friend, Basil here. *(Basil flakes out).*

How Are Things in Auchterturra?

Tune: *How Are Things in Glocamorra?*

Exile.   I'm in Hong Kong,
But nostalgia's strong.
I'd like a crack
With someone back
Where I belong.

Brrrr, Brrrr.

Local.   The phone for me.
Wonder fa't can be.
Hello – fa's there?
This is Auchtertur –
Ra 213.

Exile.   Hi, there! It's me . . .

How are things in Auchterturra?
In the post office across the square
Is there still the Thursday morning queue
Of old folk who
Draw their pensions there?

Local.   Things his changed in Auchterturra,
Now there's rural deprivation here.
The post office that once you prized's
Been rationalised –
It wis closed last year.

Exile.   Is the chemist always open
Any hour of night or day?

Local.   We hinna had a chemist since last May.
And baith my quines is in the fem'ly way.

Exile.   Is Tam Wilson still the bobby?

Local.   Well, we hinna got a bobby noo.
The p'lice station's a craft shop rin
By an Englishmin
Wi' a great big plum in his moo.

Exile. And the bank? The trusty Clydesdale?

Local. It's gone!

Exile. What? That's a sin!
So what do people keep their money in?

Local. Well, a'body has tae hae a biscuit tin.

Exile. Things have changed in Auchterturra.
But does the train still wend its way,
Leaving Rhynie just on 9 o'clock
And reaching Auch-
Terturra by mid-day?

Local. There's nae trains tae Auchterturra.
Dr. Beeching fairly saw tae that
So ye really need a motor car
Tae travel far,
Because the buses have –
Here's the laugh an' a' –
Been ta'en aff an' a'.

Exile. And the hospital?

Local. Converted!
Intae thirty time-share flats.
It wis bull-dozed, leavin' jist the vestibule,
On the very day the Cooncil closed the school.

Exile. Rural services are going.

Local. An' the powers that be jist dinna care.
The phone is all that's left tae go-

(Light on Local goes out)

Exile. Hello, hello –
Auchterturra – are you there?

Arrival

Alec is seen seated at home reading a newspaper and dipping into a large jar almost full of sweets. Norman appears on the doorstep and rings the bell. Alec answers the door.

A.   God! If it's nae yersel, Norman! Ye're a stranger. Come in.

N.   No, I'm nae comin' in. *(His speech is slow and lugubrious).*

A.   Oh, come in.

N.   No, I'm nae comin' in. I'm deliverin' election leaflets the nicht and I jist thocht I would ring yer bell. *(He hands Alec a leaflet)*

A.   Oh, but I'm affa gled ye did, Norman. So, ye're on the election leaflets the nicht. Very good. *(He screws up the leaflet without reading it)* Come in.

N.   No, I'm nae comin' in. I hinna time tae come in. I'm in an affa hurry.

A.   Oh, come in. We hinna seen ye this whilie. I wis just sayin' tae Mary at teatime, 'I hinna seen Norman this whilie. I hope he's weel enough.'

N.   Oh, I'm fine, thanks, aye. Feelin' a lot better since the doctor changed my peels.

A.   Oh! Has the doctor changed yer peels? We didna ken that, Norman. We'll need tae hear a' aboot that. Come in.

N.   No, I'm nae comin' in.

A.   I wis hearin' aboot yer aul' auntie in Aiberdeen, Norman. She hisna been affa weel. I wis affa sorry tae hear that, Norman.

N.   Auntie Betty, aye. Puir Betty. Mind you, she's in the best place.

A.   The new hospital?

N.   The aul' cemetery.

A.   Losh be here! Auntie Betty awa'? That surely couldna be richt?

N.   Well, they beeried her. Mind you, she was wintin' awa'.

A.   Wintin' awa'?

N.   Wintin' awa'.

A.   Wintin' awa'.

N.   Aye, the last time I went tae see her, oh me, she was affa doon.

A.   Affa doon?

N.   Affa doon.

A.   Affa doon . . . Oh well Norman, if you couldna cheer her up, she was better awa'. She was a good age though, was she, Norman?

N.   Aichty-sivven.

A.   Aichty-sivven, was she?

N.   Aichty-sivven past January.

A.   January.

N.   The twenty-sivventh.

A.   The twenty-sivventh.

N. If I get as lang as her, I'll be affa happy.

A. Oh Norman, ye'll be laughin' . . . Come in.

N. No, I'm nae comin' in! . . . I said I would be hame by ten o'clock tae mak Tibbie's cocoa.

A. Norman, it's only half-past-six. Come in.

N. No, I'm nae comin' in. I'm feart tae come in!

A. Feart tae come in?

N. Aye, last time I wis here I got an affa row fae Mary for keepin' ye oot o' yer bed.

A. But Norman, Mary's nae here. She's awa' oot tae her whist. Now, come in.

N. Is Mary nae in?

A. No, Norman, there's jist me an' a big jar o' jubejubes.

N. Are you tellin me, that Mary's oot, you're in there wi' a big jar o' jubejubes, an' we're stannin' on this caul' doorstep?

A. Aye. Now come in.

N. God, I thocht ye'd never ask.

Departure

Some time later, Alec and Norman are standing at the front door. Alec is holding a big jar containing only a few jubejubes.

A. Are ye sure ye winna hae anither jubejube, Norman?

N. No thanks, Alec, I'll hae tae awa'.

A. Oh ye're nae awa'? Hae anither jubejube.

N. No thanks, no, I've had enough jubejubes.

A. Enough jubejubes?

N. Aye, I get affa easy scunnered o' jubejubes.

A. D'ye nae like my jubejubes, Norman?

N. Aye, I like them fine, but I dinna think we should've gone on tae that second jar. Naw, I'll hae tae awa'.

A. Oh, ye're nae awa'. Hae another jubejube.

N. No, no!

A. Norman, they'll dae ye far mair gweed than that fancy peels ye got fae the doctor.

N. No, no, 'at peels has made a big difference.

A. A big difference?

N. A big difference tae me 'at peels. Afore I started takin' them, I jist had nae zip at a'.

A. Well, ye'd never ken that noo! Ye're jist the life and soul o' the party, Norman . . . Hae anither jubejube.

N. No, no. No, I'll hae tae awa'. I'll get murdered fan I get hame.

A. Awa'! Tibbie'll be in her bed.

N. No, she'll still be up.

A. Waitin' up for ye?

N. Waitin' up for her cocoa.

A. At three o'clock in the mornin', Norman . . . Ye're nae awa'.

N. Aye I'll hae tae awa'. I've just minded somethin' else!

A. Fit's that, Norman?

N. I've anither twa hunner election leaflets tae deliver.

(Norman departs)

A. *(Calling upstairs)* Mary, that's Norman awa'. God, I thocht I would never get rid o' him!

Ye're a stranger Mode of address to a very close friend.

Doctor Vet doing a homer in Auchterturra.

Changed my peels Got me oot o' the surgery afore I could cough.

Wintin' awa' Keen to turn up one's toes.

'REPUTATIONS'

Public reputations Are of—ten wrong— We've got some re—ve—la——tions To real—ly blow your mind———. Rea—gan's real—ly youthful ———, Cher—nen—ko's in the pink ———. The Ay—a—tol—lah Kho—mei—ni Tak's a hell—u—va drink ———.

ALL BUT LAST VERSE

Reputations

Public reputations
Are often wrong, you'll find.
We've got some revelations
To really blow your mind.
Reagan's really youthful,
Chernenko's in the pink,
The Ayatollah Khomeini
Tak's a helluva drink.

David Owen votes Conservative,
And David Steel as well;
Neil Kinnock likes Mrs. Thatcher
And so does Tam Dalyell.
Tony Benn's the darling
Of the Tory Press,
Boy George is a sergeant-major
In the SAS.

Mick Jagger does embroidery,
Cliff Richard's ayewis fu',
Pavarotti and Domingo
Are members of The Who.
John Travolta's learnin'
Tae dae a modern waltz,
Kojak wears a wig,
And Esther Rantzen's teeth are false.

Jack Nicklaus plays aff twenty
At oor local course,
Lester Piggot is allergic
To every kind of horse.
John McEnroe's a charmer
Who never wins a set;
Martina Navratilova
Keeps fa'in' ower the net.

Looking back through history
The legends melt awa' –
The fiery revolution'ries
Were nae like that at a';
Lenin was a capitalist,
Gandhi wore a suit,
Chairman Mao was the owner
Of a Chinese cairry-oot.

Pope John Paul the Second
Is a Rangers fan,
Sylvester Stallone is gay
And Dolly Parton is a man.
But the strangest reputation
Is the one that Scotland's got:
When folk sing *Scotland the Brave*.
We say 'Scotland the What?'

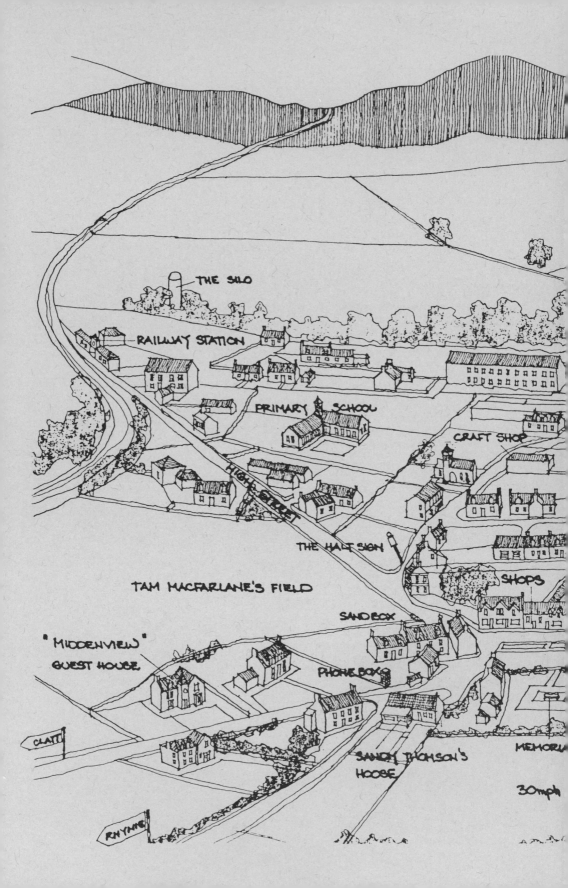

THE SILO

RAILWAY STATION

PRIMARY SCHOOL

HIGH STREET

CRAFT SHOP

THE HALT SIGN

SHOPS

TAM MACFARLANE'S FIELD

SANDBOX

"MIDDENVIEW" GUEST HOUSE

PHONE BOX

CLATT

SANDY THOMSON'S HOOSE

MEMORIAL

30mph

RHYNIE